COELEVATE

COELEVATE

HOW TO UNLOCK
BUSINESS GROWTH AND
CONSUMER VALUE
WITH STRATEGIC
PARTNERSHIPS

RICHARD
EZEKIEL

RILEY BUSINESS
NEW YORK | SAN FRANCISCO

To my parents, who gave me the gift of dreams
and the ability to realize them.

For my wife, my confidante, my love.

For my kids, who inspire me to take on new challenges,
thanks for laughing at my jokes.

To you, dear reader, for making this journey worthwhile.

co | ′kō

1. with; together; equally; jointly

2. one that is associated in an action with another; fellow; partner

el·e·vate | ′e-lə-′vāt

1. to raise or lift up someone or something to a higher position or impressive level

2. to improve morally, intellectually, or culturally

CONTENTS

FOREWORD

In 1972, shortly after Ted Dabney and I founded Atari, we hired our first employee, Allan Alcorn. Al was a brilliant engineer and computer scientist, but he didn't yet have experience with video games so I gave him an easy project to start. I told him we had a contract with General Electric because I wanted him to put his best effort into the game, but that wasn't true. There was no contract, and I didn't expect the game to go anywhere. It was meant to be a training exercise, a chance for Al to learn how to swim before we chucked him into the deep end.

"It's the simplest game," I told him. "One moving spot, two paddles, score digits." The game was, of course, Pong.

As soon as Alcorn showed us the prototype, we knew we had

a great game on our hands. A game is nothing without players, though. We believed it could be a profitable product, but we needed to test it first. We installed the prototype at a local bar, Andy Capp's Tavern. We'd previously supplied the bar with pinball machines, so we already had a good working relationship with the bar's owner, Bill Gaddis. It was a partnership, albeit unofficial, one of many that helped me achieve success in my career.

The first few nights, the game quickly gained popularity. Just a week and a half after we installed the machine, though, Gaddis phoned us, upset. The game had stopped working properly. When we went to investigate, we quickly identified the problem. The game had been too popular. It was overflowing with quarters, causing it to jam up. The test was a success, and that "simplest game" not only made a name for us at Atari but helped to establish the entire video game industry.

In those early days when we were building Atari, we had no roadmap. There were no processes or frameworks to guide us, and we broke rules faster than we could make them. Our strategy was just to out-innovate everyone else. That meant we had to get scrappy and to make things up as we went.

While there were no hard-and-fast rules, over the years, a common theme emerged: everything always came back to people. The simple truth is that you cannot succeed alone. Many of the most important growth moments at Atari and at my other companies came through partnerships, from friendly relationships with bar owners to licensing agreements with distributors to acquisitions.

Today more than ever, partnering has become essential. AI is advancing so rapidly that we can no longer fully predict the future. I can't say what education, jobs, or business will look like in another five, ten, or twenty years. What's everlasting, though, is human creativity, specifically collaborative creativity. Partnerships are and will continue to be a key competitive advantage.

We face a multi-axis problem: serving customers whose expectations keep rising, competing in markets that evolve at lightning speed, and navigating a landscape of potential partners that could unlock new growth opportunities or end up being a waste of time and resources. No company operates in a vacuum. To succeed, you must understand your full ecosystem: customers, competitors, and collaborators. Then you must identify and build the right partnerships to solve the multi-axis problem.

Today, the fundamentals haven't changed, but the game has. The stakes are higher, the tech is smarter, the playing field is global—and the partnerships are more complex. You need new skills, new strategies and tactics, and, above all, a new mindset. This is what *COELEVATE* provides. Richard doesn't just champion the power of partnerships—he gives you a flexible, proven method to build them successfully. His advice isn't theoretical either. It's drawn from decades of experience. He's worked across industries and seen firsthand what it takes to create partnerships that have a real impact. He shares the right questions to ask, the pitfalls to avoid, and dozens of helpful exercises and best practices.

If you're not partnering—or if you're not partnering as effectively as you could be—it's time to start. Because the future doesn't belong to the companies that go it alone. It belongs to those who build the right partnerships, at the right time, for the right reasons.

A lot of people have ideas, but there are few who decide to do something about them now. Not tomorrow. Not next week. But today. The true entrepreneur is a doer, not a dreamer. So, what will you do? What will you build together that you could never build alone? It starts now, with *COELEVATE*.

—Nolan Bushnell

Nolan Bushnell, founder and first CEO of Atari, has been called the "Father of the Gaming Industry" and was named one of Newsweek's "50 Men Who Changed America." *He has founded more than twenty companies, including Kadabrascope, later acquired by Lucasfilm, which became Pixar. He was the recipient of Sequoia Capital's first ever investment and created the first Silicon Valley tech incubator, Catalyst. He was also the first and only person to hire Steve Jobs and is author of* Finding the Next Steve Jobs *and* Shaping the Future of Education.

THE "PARTNERSHIP ECONOMY" IS HERE

"It's over, Rich," my boss told me. "It's looking like we're throwing in the towel. Time to start looking for another job."

My colleagues at work were all saying the same thing: our company was running out of options. Our investors said the same, and no one was happy with our results. Most people around me said I should give up.

They were wrong.

Only a year prior, ready for a new challenge, I left a Fortune 500 company to work for this early-stage tech start-up. We had an amazing CEO, a super experienced team, lots of funding, and a really cool consumer tech device that aligned well with the rise of mobile devices. But we just couldn't find traction to build our brand. Basically, we had a great product but no audience.

I believed in our product and our people, so I wasn't going to give up. I was determined to see this all the way through. I figured even if everything crashed and burned, I would learn valuable lessons. I also knew that often, when the going gets tough, that's when the best ideas come.

All we needed was one great idea. It just so happened that I had one. Our big issue was our lack of audience. One of our hardware suppliers, on the other hand, had a large audience and a well-known brand, but they were struggling to innovate and meet the evolving needs of their customers. Partnering would be a win-win. We would be able to reach a big audience using their marketing and sales channels, and they would be able to offer a cutting-edge product and stay relevant in a rapidly changing market.

I came up with the idea over a weekend. Within a week, we'd developed the proposal: our partner would handle the hardware, and we would handle the software. Within two weeks, we'd made a demo. Within a month, the deal was complete.

Not long after that, while I was shopping at Costco with my family, I stopped dead in my tracks, on the verge of tears. There in front of me, on the shelves of one of the nation's biggest retailers, was our product. The long hours, the stress and uncertainty, the drive and determination to make the partnership work—it had all culminated in this.

The product sold well, and a few months later, our partner was so pleased that they decided to acquire our company. That's when I actually cried. It was hard to believe how far things had turned around and how quickly. We'd gone from the brink of collapse to the pinnacle of success, and it was all thanks to a creative partnership idea.

This is the power of strategic partnerships. They can change a company's entire trajectory. They can make the impossible possible.

THE GROWTH PROBLEM

Nearly every business has the same goal: to grow. If your business is not growing enough to at least keep pace with inflation, it's dying.

So, what's your growth plan?

If you're like most companies, it probably involves some combination of marketing, releasing new products and services, cutting costs, and raising prices—a.k.a., you plan to internally drive the growth you need. That can work, for a while at least.

To build a great and enduring company, it's not as simple as aspiring to be the next Google, Apple, or Nvidia. You need a plan to create indispensable value for customers. I'm not saying you shouldn't dream big or have a North Star for your business, but when the available options to elevate your strategic position are extremely limited or require an insurmountable amount of time or money, you need to think differently.

The reality is that things are tough out there for businesses. Over the last decade, transformative technologies have driven an evolution of the internet from Web 1.0 (the read-only web with the beginnings of e-commerce) to 2.0 (social networks, "mobile-first," and cloud-driven computing) to 3.0 (decentralized data architectures and edge computing infrastructure). This has resulted in new businesses being created at a breakneck pace. And now with AI being the next frontier, business growth must happen faster than ever. According to a recent Global Entrepreneurship Monitor (GEM) national report, more than *100 million* start-ups are launched globally every year. Data from Flourish Ventures also points to an increase in the number of companies started post-pandemic, with about 5.5 million new start-ups in the US in 2023, an 8 percent increase from 2022. Also, tech companies grew 2.3 times more since the pandemic than non-tech companies. The increase in new businesses has made it difficult for companies to differentiate themselves while also making it critical that they go to market quickly.

While many businesses are started, few survive. That GEM report found that of all small businesses started in 2014, 80 percent made it to the second year, 70 percent made it to the third year, 62 percent made it to the fourth year, and only 56 percent made it to the fifth year. In other words, the difference between success and failure can seem like a coin flip. In addition, the lifespan of large, successful companies has never been shorter. Take a look at these stats from Innosight about turnover in the S&P 500:

▸ In 1965, the average tenure of companies on the S&P 500 was thirty-three years. By 1990, it was twenty years. It's forecast to shrink to twelve years by 2027.

▸ About 50 percent of the S&P 500 will be replaced over the next ten years.

Many renowned companies have fallen off of the S&P 500 list: Eastman Kodak, US Steel, National Semiconductor, and the New York Times. If even these companies, with incredible financial resources and human talent, struggle with maintaining growth, it's obviously a tricky problem.

THE PARTNERSHIP ECONOMY: PARTNERSHIPS ARE TAKING OVER THE WORLD

Of course, there are success stories as well. New companies to the S&P 500 list include Uber, Lululemon, Under Armour, and Netflix. Guess what all those companies have in common: *strategic partnerships*. Uber partnered with Spotify, Lululemon with Peloton, Under Armour with Dwayne "The Rock" Johnson and Stephen Curry, and Netflix with every consumer electronics company you could imagine. If you start looking for them, you'll realize that partnerships are *everywhere* and come in every shape and size.

One hundred years ago, the way companies did business was very different from today. Across nearly every industry—from food and beverage to automobiles to film production—businesses tended to be vertically integrated, meaning they built and operated everything on their own. Often this was done out of necessity. Anytime a new industry is created, there is an incubation period in which companies need to develop vertically integrated structures for end-to-end development because the needed components simply do not exist yet. With time, though, as competition increases, the industry becomes more specialized, and it no longer makes sense for a single company to do it all. Instead, it is more cost effective and efficient for them to seek out the strengths and expertise of other companies in technology, marketing, and talent.

Thus *the partnership economy* was born. The partnership economy refers to the wealth, resources, and opportunities that are generated through strategic relationships between companies.

Here's the real kicker. More and more, "the partnership economy" is simply becoming "*the* economy." Partnerships are becoming the foundation of how businesses operate. They are not limited to a single industry or type of company. Almost any business can—and, I would argue, *should*—partner.

THE POWER OF PARTNERSHIPS

So now, when you think about the growth of your company, do you really want to risk going at it alone? You're running out of time, the clock is ticking, and the stakes have never been higher. To solve the challenges customers and our communities face, we must accelerate and innovate together, bringing the best of our strengths to address the world's biggest problems—and your business goals. I'm not saying you need to solve global poverty or stop global warming, but imagine an idealistic world that brings together a structured win-win system and process to ensure all parties involved maintain what is important to them while contributing to the greater good. Partnerships don't mean you will lose control or be at the mercy of another company. I will help you see other perspectives on partnerships in which they can be a catalyst for change, growth, and speed. I ask you to put any prenotions aside as you read and think through the ideas brought forth in this book.

As the African proverb says, "If you want to go far, go together." If you want to survive and thrive in our modern economy, you need partnerships. Through strategic partnerships, you can:

▶ Accelerate growth and speed to market

▶ Offset costs

▶ Increase your audience

▶ Gain new distribution channels

▶ Improve your brand image

▶ Access new skill sets, knowledge, and expertise

▶ Enter and compete in new markets and regions

▶ Create new product and service offerings for customers

▶ Drive innovation and offer unique competitive advantages

At this point, you might be wondering, "If partnerships are so great, why don't more companies do them?" Simple answer: they may not know how. A lot of time, effort, and creativity goes on behind the scenes to bring partnerships to life. Throughout my career, I've heard from many business leaders that partnerships are "squishy," meaning they are really hard to track and predict. While engineering and sales have clear tools and processes, partnering is more like an art form. There is a science to it as well, though.

Maybe you've never tried to do a partnership before and feel lost, unsure where to start. Or maybe you have tried and the partnership crashed and burned or sputtered out before providing real results. What you need is a clear process. That's why I wrote this book: to demystify the puzzling and often-misunderstood art and science of successful partnerships, providing a predictable and proven path to unlock growth and differentiation to accelerate your business.

A METHOD TO THE MADNESS

I've worked in partnerships and business development in Silicon Valley for more than twenty years. In that time, I have been directly responsible for creating and launching over one thousand high-quality partnerships. I've worked with all kinds of businesses, from early-stage start-ups to Fortune 100 companies. These partnerships have included Netflix, Google, Meta, Pinterest, Lyft, Lime, OfferUp, and more than one hundred other companies. I was also previously part of the Andreessen Horowitz team, where I was dedicated to helping founders and companies succeed, no matter their stage of growth. Some of those partnerships unlocked massive company growth and defined new industries, while others failed spectacularly. The lessons learned are what matters, and I want to share those learnings with you.

Two or more companies are needed to create a business partnership. Speaking the same language, using the same process, and aligning on and following the same partnering framework is fundamental. Otherwise, you have no map to get you both to your target destination. Think about it like the difference between a scavenger hunt and a treasure map. With a scavenger hunt, you must go through a complex and unpredictable set of events that lead to a winner (a result). With a treasure map, you have a guide for how best to get to the destination and treasure (impactful partnership outcomes). The majority of today's business partnership "scavenger hunts" are not a result of parties wanting to make these engagements complex. Rather, I believe the issue is a lack of alignment on a common language, process, and framework, as there isn't an industry accepted and recognized standard for how to develop high-impact strategic partnerships. Today, while one company or individual may have done a successful partnership in the past, don't assume that all parties involved understand or have that same experience. Many of the skills, practices, tips, and tricks related to partnerships are tribal knowledge inside of various companies. Each company has its own tribal knowledge, limited knowledge, or no knowledge at all for how to create and execute a business partnership. This book is intended to present a common language, process, and framework that partnering companies can explore, adjust, and align on to better realize their strategic partnership.

Something I discovered early in my career is that there's not a good guidebook to strategic partnerships (trust me—I looked!). Instead, I had to learn my lessons through hard-won, on-the-job experience. Over time, I started to identify the commonalities around what works and what doesn't work, and I developed the Co-Elevate Method, a method to guide you through the madness of the partnering journey, with its peaks and valleys, twists and turns. Essentially, this book is my attempt to create the guidebook I wish I had, so you don't have to go through the same trial and error I did. It's a combination of proven business development (BD) methods and the insights I gained from hundreds of real-life partnerships.

I've written this book with the beginner in mind. If you've never done a partnership, this book will take you through the entire process, with a focus on how to establish successful partnership relationships. Whether you're a CEO looking for new growth opportunities for your company, you're still in school or fresh out of college just starting your career, or you're an experienced manager looking to pivot into partnering and BD, this book can get you up to speed on important partnering tips, tricks, and methodologies. Even if you have been doing partnerships and BD for years and already know a lot of the information in this book, I hope you pick up new strategies and ways of thinking about partnering.

Whatever your level of experience, you may disagree with parts of this book. That's okay. In fact, it's encouraged! Partnering isn't an exact science. The Co-Elevate Method is not a guarantee of success or a formula you can follow exactly. Every situation is unique due to the product area, the personalities involved, and other nuances. There are just so many things that are unpredictable. But the Co-Elevate Method provides a foundation so that, using your judgment, you can navigate through your unique situation and apply the tools and strategies that are helpful. Also know that the Co-Elevate Method isn't a one-and-done process. It is about finding your company's groove with partnership development and making it a habit and part of how your company operates. As partnering becomes part of your company culture, successful, high-quality partnerships will become more predictable, repeatable, and scalable.

The book is organized according to the different stages of the Co-Elevate Method:

▸ **Stage 0, The Partnership Runway:** The foundational knowledge you need to establish successful partnerships

▸ **Stage 1, Explore—The Big Idea:** How to figure out your partnership "flight plan" and choose the partners to get you to your desired destination

▸ **Stage 2, Align—Taking Flight:** How to engage your prospects and close the deal, getting the metaphorical partnership plane off the ground

▸ **Stage 3, Execute—Gaining Altitude:** How to manage the partnership in order to achieve success and get the partnership plane to cruising altitude

▶ **Stage 4, Grow—Reaching New Heights:** How to increase the scope of an initial partnership and repeat the partnering process so you have not just a single partnership plane but a whole fleet

A new era of business is upon us, so let's embrace what partnerships can do. Let's expand your company into new markets and create amazing new value for consumers. Let's elevate your thinking outside of your company's walls. Let's develop your Co-Elevate Partnership.

STAGE 0

THE PARTNERSHIP RUNWAY

CHAPTER 1

TO PARTNER OR NOT TO PARTNER

"Watch Whatever, Whenever"

"TV Your Way"

Heard of these advertising slogans? They could be from the same company, right? Well, they're not. In fact, they are from two different decades! But both slogans are about providing consumers with benefits around "time-shifting" television, since not until the 2000s did we have other options beyond "appointment TV," where you had to sit down on your couch at a specific time to watch your favorite show when it aired.

"Watch Whatever, Whenever" was a slogan for Sony's Betamax, the first VCR (videocassette recorder) innovation brought to the consumer market, first launched in the '70s and made more available to consumers in the early to mid '80s. I grew up with a Sony Betamax video camera as a kid, and I loved it. It was before the VHS (Video Home System) format, which was created by JVC. Betamax was the superior format over VHS with better resolution and sound quality, along with higher-quality construction. VCRs, in general, were not bad for popping in a prerecorded video and playing it, but programming it to record a show? No way! They were considerably complex to program. But VHS ended up winning out over Betamax.

"TV Your Way" is a slogan from the first commercially successful DVR (digital video recorder): TiVo. TiVo was first introduced in 1999 at the Consumer Electronics Show (CES). Fast-forward to 2005 and TiVo had the best features and an easier-to-use user interface than any other DVR at the time. In comparison, DISH Network's DVR had known bugs and would lock up, lose audio, have pixelated video, and even lose timers for recording. Yet DISH Network's DVR had the most users.

Both Betamax and TiVo's DVR were superior in their value to consumers, but competitors with lower-quality features or harder-to-use products won. There are a lot of reasons why they both failed, but I'd argue that the fundamental reason is the same: they didn't partner.

JVC did two important things with VHS that Sony didn't do with Betamax:

1. JVC worked with other consumer electronics manufacturers and licensed their VHS tech and logo so others could produce VHS players. Sony was the only company to create Betamax devices, and they continued to go at it alone versus embracing a partnering approach in the early stages.

2. JVC secured licensed content on VHS—specifically, post-theater releases, full-length movies, and specialized or niche video content. The availability of compelling content that consumers wanted drove the widespread adoption of VHS.

Likewise, TiVo missed out on key partnership opportunities that could have propelled them to the top of the DVR market. The challenge was that to get TiVo's solution you needed to buy a separate device. For DISH, you already had a DVR inside of your DISH set-top box. The DVR was a feature integrated with your subscription to DISH for an additional monthly charge. You could access it from your existing set-top box remote, and it was in the same user interface too.

In fact, both Betamax and TiVo did end up partnering with others eventually. Betamax later licensed their player tech and partnered with other consumer electronics manufacturers, but it was too late. VHS was already the mainstream. TiVo later partnered with TV service operators, most notably Comcast, but again, it was too late. On-demand video streaming was coming onto the scene, and so recording live television was no longer as compelling to consumers.

Looking back years later, it's easy to say that Betamax and TiVo *could have* and *should have* partnered sooner with others to win. Many now recognize the value of partnerships and pursuing them at the right time. Per the PwC Global CEO Survey, 85 percent of C-level business leaders view partnerships as "essential" or "important" to their business's future. *The Harvard Business Review* further found that the number of strategic partnerships is growing by 25 percent a year, accounting for nearly one-third of many companies' revenue and value.

What about your company? How do you know whether you should partner or not? You don't want to get out-partnered by others or what I like to call "Betamaxed." In this chapter, we'll look at exactly what partnerships are and why you should or shouldn't partner.

WHAT IS A STRATEGIC PARTNERSHIP?

Not all partnerships are created equal. A lot of companies misuse the term *partner,* and partnership can mean different things to different people. When I use the term *partnership* in this book, I am referring specifically to *Co-Elevate Partnerships.*

Co-Elevate Partnership: A strategic long-term relationship in which both parties mutually benefit using the method outlined in this book.

The key word here is *strategic.* In fact, you may hear such partnerships referred to as *strategic alliances,* but this term has fallen out of use in recent years, so in this book, I will instead use the terms *strategic partnerships* or *Co-Elevate Partnerships.* Many companies call any long-term relationship a partnership. For example, I've often seen preferred suppliers called "partners." While this is a long-term relationship that is valuable to both parties, it's not quite a partnership. Preferred supplier relationships are typically sales-oriented relationships, with a primary goal being price optimization. A partnership requires collaboration and working together toward strategic goals.

Let's say you sell pens. In a supplier relationship, you're just trying to buy ink you want at the lowest cost. In a partnership, you might work with the company that makes ink to develop a new innovative pen together under a new model name, with the goal of increasing writing accuracy and legibility while reducing hand fatigue. Both companies enlist a notable orthopedic doctor specializing in hand, wrist, and elbow care to be a key design advisor. The result is a pen that integrates a new, long-lasting, smooth-writing ink combined with new roller ball tip and weighted soft-grip design. See the difference? Partnerships are transformative, not just transactional. Pro tip: If you see anything about a request for proposal (RFP), request for information (RFI), or request for quote (RFQ), that's a signal you're dealing with a supplier relationship, not a true partnership, but you may have an opportunity to transition to a strategic partnership through this type of process (we'll cover that later).

A true strategic partnership is a synergy. It is two (or more) companies coming together to do something they couldn't do alone. A strategic partnership requires:

▸ A vision and partnership idea

▸ An impact on priorities (reward)

▸ Investment (cost, resources, time)

▸ Planning and management systems

▸ Trust, Transparency, Communication

The first two elements are the basis for *why* to have a partnership. The remaining three are *how* to manage the partnership. Each facet must be shared between the parties to truly reflect the nature of this more intimate and personalized relationship. All together, these traits form the foundation for developing and maintaining a strong and viable partnership.

TOP REASONS TO PARTNER

So how do you know if *you* should partner? There are five big indicators that a partnership could help your company.

#1: YOUR GROWTH HAS STALLED OR IS TOO SLOW

The number one reason to partner is to supercharge your growth.

There are two ways to grow: organic growth and inorganic growth. Organic growth is internally driven growth, while inorganic growth is externally driven, through acquisitions or partnerships.

Organic growth includes things like word-of-mouth marketing, product range expansion, and internal new product development. While organic growth activities can be effective—and must be continued for a company to survive—they have some drawbacks:

▸ Organic growth takes **time** and **money.** Organic growth initiatives can require you to build a new team, allocate new budgets, and then execute over months or years. Even then, the initiative might fail, or growth will only happen incrementally. Especially if you have to consider board members and shareholders (who usually prefer more rapid growth of revenues and profits), organic growth timelines and costs might not cut it.

▸ Organic growth can be **unpredictable**. It is often dependent on factors outside of your control, like competitors, shifts in customer needs and behavior, and the growth of the overall market. Since there's so much you can't control, organic growth tends to be riskier than inorganic methods done right.

▸ Organic growth has **limits**. You can hit a point where organic growth is maxed out. Especially if your business is already an industry leader, it can be hard to continue building market share through organic growth alone.

Partnerships aren't foolproof. They also take time and money, and there's still risk involved. However, the costs and risks are simultaneously mitigated by and shared with your partner (assuming the partnership is set up that way, which I recommend). Strategic partnerships are designed so that companies can use each other's strengths and offset each other's weaknesses. By partnering with a company that has already proven success or aptitude in a certain area, you take some of the unknowns out of the equation and unlock a more predictable path to success. Since you also share the costs, either in money or time or both, the growth is not only more predictable, but can also be faster and cheaper. And it's nearly limitless.

#2: YOU'RE TRYING TO EXPAND TO A NEW AUDIENCE OR REGION

Often, when a company's growth hits a plateau, it's because they've already maximized their audience. To grow further, they need to increase their audience, either by targeting a different demographic or expanding into a new region. Both of these can be challenging. There's a steep learning curve because you're trying to do something you've never done before. Partnering with a company that already understands the target demographic's needs or the target region's cultural idiosyncrasies is a shortcut to success. With the right partner, you can break into a new demographic, region, and industry, and you can partner as many times as you like.

For example, when Evernote wanted to expand into Japan, they could have chosen to do it on their own. However, it would have been a hard uphill battle. They would have had to navigate language barriers, government restrictions, distribution complexities, and a host of cultural nuances around how products are developed, marketed, and received in the country. Instead, they opted to partner with Japanese companies, Nikkei and DOCOMO, which allowed them to successfully launch in the country and build a sustainable business in Japan, growing it to be their second-largest market after the US.

#3: YOU WANT TO DRIVE INNOVATION

In a survey of executives from ninety-one companies with revenue greater than $1 billion across more than twenty industries, Innosight asked, "What is your organization's biggest obstacle to transform in response to market change and disruption?" About 40 percent of survey respondents blamed "day-to-day decisions that essentially pay the bills but undermine our stated strategy to change." The next most popular answer, at 24 percent, was "lack of a coherent vision for the future." In other words, the survey results highlight how hard it is for leaders to break free of organizational inertia—the existing mindsets and processes in organizations. Yet that's what has to be done if you want to build an enduring company. You can't rely on what you've always done forever. You have to innovate.

Innovation means creating something new. One of the easiest ways to do that is to add something new into the mix—a.k.a., a partner. With a partner in the equation, you have new resources, knowledge, and talent to draw on, which opens up far more possibilities for innovation. A partner shakes up the status quo and helps you break out of organizational inertia.

#4: YOU LACK CERTAIN SKILLS AND CAPABILITIES

Many times, the reason companies don't innovate isn't because they don't want to or don't have good ideas. It's simply that they don't have the needed skills or capabilities. This can take many forms. Sometimes it's a lack of the right people to achieve a certain goal. For example, a company might not have in-house teams capable of building a certain technical product feature or service that would benefit their customers. Other times it might be an organizational capability that is missing, like poor brand awareness or limited sales channels.

In today's day and age, it's just not possible to do it all by yourself. Would you build your own cloud service to stand up your website and IT operations? Or build your own advertising platform to deliver your promotions to your users? Or create a social network to engage your target customers? You get the point. Rather than trying to be all things to all customers, most companies can only be excellent at one thing (or a few things). Instead of investing a ton of time and money into building certain skills and capabilities, it can be far more effective and efficient to partner with a company that already excels in those areas. The essence of a great partnership is to combine each other's expertise in order to provide a unique experience for your customers.

#5: YOU'RE EXPERIENCING START-UP OR NEW INITIATIVE STRUGGLES

It's hard to be a start-up, whether you're starting a brand-new company or a new initiative within an existing company. The stats can be downright depressing. Some sources, like Startup Genome's *2022 Global Startup Ecosystem Report*, cite that as many as 90 percent of start-ups end up failing. Often, partnerships are exactly what new companies need in order to break into their market and find firmer footing.

In a 2021 report, CB Insights identified the top reasons start-ups fail, based on an analysis of 101 start-up postmortems. Let's break down the top four reasons, with examples of how partnerships could help. (Note: these are also relevant for new initiatives within existing companies.)

1. **No market need:** A lack of market need is often not actually a lack of market need but a lack of the proper positioning. For example, maybe your company developed a really great insulation technology to keep liquids hot or cold. If you try to sell your own insulated bottles, you might struggle, because there are already lots of insulation products on the market. You could mistakenly believe there's no market need, even if your insulation technology is better than others' and could provide more value to customers. If you partnered with a company like YETI or Stanley to use your insulation technology in their products, then all of a sudden there's a market need. Your insulation technology gives them a product advantage, and their brand and distribution channel give you access to their audience in the market segment.

2. **Ran out of cash:** A big benefit of partnerships is you can often do more with less, because you are sharing the costs with a partner. If you're trying to pay for *everything* yourself—from product development to marketing—you're going to run out of cash more quickly. In the

previous example, if you want to sell your own insulated bottles, you're going to have to spend *a lot* on marketing to get on people's radar. If you partner with a well-known brand like YETI or Stanley, you can instead look to use *their* marketing investments for your product.

3. **Not the right team:** This goes back to the #4 reason to partner. Sometimes you don't have the right skills and capabilities within your company, and it may not be feasible to hire full-time positions for what you need. Partners can fill the gap.

4. **Got outcompeted:** Competition is a top reason for partnering. There are more companies today than ever before. (According to Statista, in 2023, there were an estimated 359 million companies worldwide.) The only way to succeed is to find competitive advantages. With so many other companies using partnerships to be more competitive, you often have to partner as well in order to keep up. (Remember: Don't get Betamaxed.)

If you're curious, these were the next six reasons for failure:

▶ Pricing/cost issues

▶ User-unfriendly product

▶ Product without a business model

▶ Poor marketing

▶ Ignoring customers

▶ Product mistimed

Arguably, partnerships could help with not just these but several of the other issues start-ups and new initiatives commonly face. The fundamental purpose of a Co-Elevate Partnership is to find a partner who offsets your company's weaknesses and accelerates paths to innovation and growth.

TOP REASONS NOT TO PARTNER

There are many great reasons to partner. Almost every company can benefit from partnering at some point in their life cycle. So the next important question to answer is "When should I *not* partner?"

Obviously, I believe in partnerships, or I wouldn't have written this book. But partnerships aren't a cure-all. They are a strategy. The question isn't whether partnerships are useful; it's whether they are useful *for your company, at a particular moment in time.*

Let's look at the big reasons you might *not* want to partner.

#1: YOU ARE STILL IN PRODUCT-BUILDING MODE

Not all companies are ready for partnerships. There are specific points in a company's journey when they are ready to engage in a partnership: (1) after there is a working product but no audience or (2) when there is a new product with an early-adopter audience that needs broader reach. In most successful partnerships, the company has already established *product-market fit,* meaning they have a product (either good or service) that satisfies a strong market demand. Their market is defined, their product fulfills a need for consumers in that market, and they have achieved some measure of success through going at it alone.

Establishing product-market fit is important because it gives you time to determine what is core (the critical differentiation of your business) and what is *context* (everything else) in your company. If you try to do partnerships before you understand what is core and what is context, you might accidentally damage or lose what makes your company so special. For example, imagine if Coca-Cola partnered with another company to manufacture their Coke formula. That would have been a disaster! The secret formula for Coke is core and a trade secret—the fact it can't be replicated is what makes Coca-Cola so special and competitive.

If you try to partner too early, when you're still in product-building mode and your product is not yet defined, your partnership is most likely doomed to fail. Even with a smart partnership idea, if the product isn't viable, the partnership won't be either. Not only is the partnership doomed to fail, but you can harm the company as well. Valuable resources, execution time, and mindshare that should be focused on getting the product right will instead be redirected to the partnership. The partnership can end up being a distraction that prevents you from creating a viable product.

Now, there are *some* cases where partnerships can be utilized in order to accelerate the path to product-market fit. One of the most notable examples is the partnership between Apple and AT&T in 2007, for the iPhone. In order for the iPhone to reach customers, Apple needed a wireless network provider. AT&T filled that role, becoming the exclusive US mobile operator for the iPhone at launch. AT&T also invested in the development of the iPhone, and the two companies had an unprecedented revenue-sharing agreement, where AT&T got a portion of iPhone sales and Apple got a portion of each iPhone customer's bill. While the partnership was developed before full product-market fit, Apple had previously demonstrated success with other products, and they had prototypes they could show AT&T. Essentially, there was enough proof of concept for both companies to sign on to the partnership, and together, they achieved product-market fit for the iPhone and mutual success.

When a partnership is fundamental to the product and needed to develop the product offering (like the earlier example of having insulation technology and partnering with another company to put it into products), it can be wise to partner early. Most of the time, though, the purpose of partnerships is to be a catalyst for growth, and you first need a good product that meets a customer need.

If you haven't achieved product-market fit yet, don't worry. There's still value for you in this book. It's always good to look ahead and plan for partnerships. The initial assessment stages of partnerships can be done without product-market fit. You simply don't want to start engaging with potential partners until you have a proven product.

#2: YOUR INDUSTRY ISN'T MATURE ENOUGH

In addition to product-market fit, you also need something I call *partnership-market fit,* meaning there is a problem or need in a market segment that can be addressed through a partnership. There are three things needed for partnership-market fit:

1. Your company has a problem or need that could be solved with a partnership.

2. There are target prospects that could solve your problem and that could also benefit from a partnership.

3. The partnership would fill a gap or need in a market area, benefiting customers.

If your industry isn't mature enough, even if you have product-market fit, you might not have partnership-market fit. Remember in the introduction when I talked about the "incubation period" for new industries? When an industry is new, often the needed partnering solutions don't exist yet, and the needs for partnering may not be fully clear.

Take Ford as an example. You've undoubtedly heard of the Model T—the first mass-affordable automobile that revolutionized the industry. The Model T is famous for its use and optimization of the assembly line, but partnering also played a key role in this vehicle's success.

Before the Model T's release in 1908, there was the Model A in 1903. The Ford Motor Company built every single part for this vehicle, including the engine. They did *not* partner, and that was the right choice. The needed suppliers were not available. There wasn't even a parts licensing model yet. Plus, Ford hadn't yet fully embraced the assembly line (which was core for them, not context), so they wouldn't know where they could most benefit from suppliers. If Ford had tried to partner at this point, I suspect they would have faced major logistical issues.

By the time of the Model T, things had changed. In order to reduce vehicle costs for consumers, Ford revolutionized the use of assembly lines and partnered with the brothers Horace and John Dodge. The Dodge brothers ran a machine shop and became a parts supplier for Ford, supplying castings, forgings, machined parts, and assemblies, including gear boxes. Ford's business and the surrounding automotive industry had matured enough to allow partnering, which contributed to the efficient, cost-effective production method of the Model T.

Basically, the point of this story is that even if *you* are ready to partner, the industry you're operating in might not be ready. In early industry development, build first and then look to partner with others. Pay particular attention to your competition, as they may be the best targets for partnerships—just as the Dodge brothers were for Ford.

#3: YOU DON'T HAVE A GOOD PARTNERSHIP IDEA

I'm going to take a wild guess here that you *want* to partner. Why else would you be spending your valuable time reading this book? However, partnering just for the sake of partnering is not always effective. Think of it like exercise. We all know that exercise is good for us, but if you go out and run a marathon without any training, you're just going to hurt yourself.

You should only partner when you have a clear partnership idea that will really move the needle for your business. A partnership is only as good as your partnering idea. If you don't have a good enough idea, then the partnership won't have much of an impact. Even if it doesn't hurt the business, it won't help enough to be a clear success, and executive teams probably won't get excited about partnering again in the future.

While you need a great partnership idea, don't worry if you don't have one right now. That's part of what this book is for. In chapter 6, "Brainstorming the Big Idea," I will take you through my brainstorming methods to help you uncover great partnership concepts for your business.

#4: YOU DON'T HAVE THE NEEDED RESOURCES TO EXECUTE A PARTNERSHIP

You also need to consider your company's capabilities. Even if you have an amazing idea, if you don't have the needed resources to execute it—whether that's time, the team, the operational expertise, or so on—then the partnership won't succeed. Sometimes it's better to wait until you have the resources you need or to explore other partnership ideas in the meantime.

TOP PARTNERING MYTHS

At this point, you hopefully have a better idea of whether to partner or not to partner. However, you might still have some doubts, especially if you're new to partnerships or have struggled to find value with them in the past. There are a lot of myths floating around about partnerships, and it's worth taking a closer look at what's fact and what's fiction.

MYTH #1: PARTNERSHIPS ARE RARELY WIN-WIN

In partnerships, one company is often larger or more well-known than the other, and it's easy to assume that the smaller, less well-known company has more to gain from the partnership. After all, the big company may have a more established brand, existing customers, and a predictable revenue stream. The smaller company might not have those, and that's exactly why they're looking to partner. Connecting with the big company's already engaged audience or positioning their brand alongside the big company's brand brings credibility and boosts the smaller company's brand to end customers and also to new prospective partners or sales targets.

If you're the smaller company, while the benefits of partnership are obvious, you may feel like you don't have anything compelling to offer in return. If you're the larger company, you may question whether it's worth it to partner at all. The bigger company might be at an evolved stage of growth where it's not about those same goals of establishing a brand, creating a revenue stream, and so on. But there *are* still benefits to partnering. Big companies need to innovate and attract new types of customers. They will be focused on optimizing operations and logistics to save on costs while exploring new growth initiatives beyond their core competencies.

There's also the flip side of this, where the partnership is seen as more beneficial to the bigger company, because they may be the ones with the capital, brand recognition, or more perceived influence in the relationship. The smaller company might feel intimidated or believe they are in a weaker position in a partner relationship.

Can partnerships be unequal? Of course! I've worked with some business development (BD) folks who actively try to create win-lose partnerships, where they're the ones winning. But that's typically a recipe for disaster in the long term. I'd argue it's not a partnership at all. We'll get into this more in the next chapter, but one of the keys to a successful partnership is that *both* parties benefit and have a say in the partnership (hence the title of this book: *Co-Elevate*). So while it's true that partnerships can be unequal, I would argue that *successful* partnerships are almost always win-win.

MYTH #2: PARTNERSHIPS GIVE AWAY THE FARM

One of the biggest fears in partnerships is that you will inadvertently sacrifice the long-term health of your business for short-term gains. Specifically, you may worry that your partner will use your ideas and your intellectual property (IP), and you'll lose control of the very thing that makes your business so special.

You will likely need to share some information in order to partner, but you don't want to give away the farm. You need guardrails in place to ensure the partnership is structured in such a way to protect your company and your IP. It's always a good idea to consult with a BD professional and a legal team to manage your risk.

MYTH #3: PARTNERSHIPS ARE GLORIFIED SALES DEALS

Many approach partnerships like glorified sales deals, but those are *not* true partnerships, not the way we are defining them in this book. In chapter 3, "Building Partnerships as a Discipline," I break down the differences and similarities between business development and sales. For now, you just need to know that traditional sales deals and processes are typically more *transactional*, while partnerships are more *strategic*.

That said, there can be some gray area. Sometimes a sales relationship can turn into a partnership. It ultimately comes down to the mindset. Is the relationship focused on money (either getting it or saving it)? Or is it focused on creating strategic value for both companies?

MYTH #4: EVERY PARTNERSHIP IS UNIQUE

Some believe that every partnership is unique, so successful partnering is not something you can easily replicate or teach. Again, there is some truth to this one. Partnerships are relationships, and so each one is unique, because there are different people and companies involved. However, there are similarities and common strategies you can draw on. It's like football. Every game will be a little different, but you have a playbook—a framework to apply to the specific scenario.

MYTH #5: ANYONE CAN BUILD SUCCESSFUL PARTNERSHIPS

People sometimes underestimate the amount of work and skill required for partnering. They think that anyone can do it, and they might even point to partnerships they've already done. To that, I would say that anyone can dance, but there's a big difference between the flailing I do at a holiday party and a professional breakdancer's performance.

Partnering is the same way. Sure, anyone could muddle through and come up with something that looks like a partnership. But to get the best results, you need a methodology and people who have developed the partnering skill set.

MYTH #6: I DON'T HAVE EXPERIENCE IN CREATING PARTNERSHIPS, SO I CAN'T LAUNCH A PARTNERSHIP

The flip side of myth #5 is the idea that only highly experienced partnering experts can do partnerships. If you don't have experience, partnering can feel overwhelming. You don't know where to start. You don't even know who to hire. Here's the thing: not everyone can do partnerships, but just about anyone can learn. It is a skill set, and skills can be developed. Throughout this book, you'll start building your partnering muscle. From there, the only way to get experience is to do partnerships. You've got this!

MYTH #7: PARTNERSHIPS AREN'T WORTH IT

This is one of the biggest myths I encounter. Many companies see partnering as optional, so they never bother exploring it. Or they will try it out but then give up because partnerships take too long or there's not a clear return on investment (ROI).

Today, if you want to build a global company with long-term success, partnering is not optional. It is a necessity. Okay, I'm sure there are exceptions, but I truly believe that partnering is core to a business's success. Sure, you can be successful without partnering, but can you be as successful as possible? I don't think so.

On a macro scale, partnerships are definitely worth it. On a micro scale, they might not be. Partnerships do take time, as well as effort and often financial investment, and you don't want to waste your resources. The Co-Elevate Method is designed to increase the probability that the partnership will have a strong positive impact on your business. Part of this is establishing upfront how you will quantitatively gauge success in the partnership.

SHOULD YOU PARTNER?

So, should you partner? Yes! But should you partner *right now*? I don't know. Ultimately, that is a question only you can answer. If you're on the fence or even leaning toward no, I encourage you to keep reading anyway. Go all the way through chapter 6, "Brainstorming the Big Idea." That will provide you with further clarity over whether and how partnerships could benefit your company. Even if you do ultimately decide not to pursue a partnership right now, you will have a better understanding of your company—its strengths, weaknesses, and needs—which will serve you well.

In the next chapter, we'll look at why partnerships fail, and I'll outline the core principles of a Co-Elevate Partnership that can lead you to successful outcomes through partnering.

CHAPTER 2

A WINNING PARTNERING METHOD

Louis Vuitton launched his brand more than 150 years ago, a luggage company that evolved into an upscale luxury brand. In 2013, Delphine Arnault, daughter of the CEO Bernard Arnault, was appointed executive VP of Louis Vuitton. She was thirty-eight years old when she took the job. Since then, the luxury brand started to focus on a younger demographic with teen-oriented marketing, innovative new products like glow-in-the-dark bags, and younger celebrity promoters like Sophie Turner. In 2017, this shift in marketing included partnering with Supreme, one of the world's coolest and exclusive streetwear brands, to design and launch a series of co-branded luxury products.

This partnership may seem like an unlikely match, but by accessing Supreme's customer base of the ultra-wealthy youth, Louis

Vuitton gained significant mindshare and market share with Generation Z (born between the mid to late 1990s and early 2010s). Most teens can't afford to spend between $1,000 and $10,000 on a Louis Vuitton bag, but likely those purchases were mostly made by their parents or grandparents. These targeted marketing efforts may also condition teen buyers to consider Louis Vuitton products once they have the funds as they get older. Supreme, meanwhile, gained credibility from working with one of the most prestigious luxury brands of all time. This was a perfectly designed partnership by both parties to tap into the modern-day zeitgeist capturing the mood and spirit of Generation Z.

Luxury fashion brands can try to engage a broader audience and distribute their brands more mass market, but if the partnership is not structured correctly—from the vision to brand alignment to pricing strategies—the outcomes may not yield the intended results. In 2012, Neiman Marcus engaged with Target and became a good example of what not to do. Industry press and customer feedback was that the collaboration created bad designs with poor quality at high prices. The items were priced higher than most of Target's items, yet the quality was the same. Before long, Target dropped prices on the collection by 70 percent. The general mismatch in the partnership strategy showed a lack of focus on who the customer is and what that customer wants. The Neiman Marcus customer experience is about browsing luxury brands that have unique designs with high quality at a high price, but the Target experience is built for the mass-market customer who is looking for great prices, from groceries to electronics to pharmacy items. Partnership mismatches like this can cause long-term damage to reputable brands. The experience that customers have with a brand builds an impression of the products and services the brand offers, creating brand affinity, or how customers emotionally connect to the brand. A poor or out-of-brand-character experience may shift brand sentiment and customer buyer behavior with it, so you need to be careful about how and who you partner with. It can make or break your company and brand. Based on Target's more recent partnerships and innovations—like Starbucks drive-up delivery and shop-in-shops with Apple, Disney, and Levi's—it looks as though Target has learned from past experience and is building their partnering muscle.

There's no point sugarcoating it: partnerships are extremely difficult to get right. There are huge benefits to be had, but there are also risks. Even when partnerships appear to be similar on the surface—like two different high-end fashion brands engaging in partnerships to broaden their customer audiences—the results can be very different. Statistics from KPMG, PwC, and Gartner all point to a troubling fact: 70 percent of partnerships fail after two years. The big question is: Why? The even bigger question is: How do you become part of the 30 percent of partnerships that succeed?

WHY DO PARTNERSHIPS FAIL?

Not all partnerships work. If you want to succeed, you first need to know what pitfalls to avoid. Here are some of the top mistakes I often see.

#1: NOT HAVING A SHARED OBJECTIVE

Partnerships require time and effort, so it's important to have a shared objective: a *why* for the partnership.

Sometimes, you might think you have a shared objective when you don't. When and how was the objective discussed and agreed upon and by whom? Have things changed over time? How strong is that shared objective to both companies involved? It may be critical to you and your company, but is it to your prospect?

The *why* for the partnership needs to be compelling to both parties, and it needs to be explicitly stated.

#2: WEAK, UNBALANCED, OR VAGUE INCENTIVES

A big part of the *why* for the partnership is about incentives. What does each company get out of the partnership? There are three ways partnerships go wrong with incentives:

▶ **Weak incentives:** If the benefits don't outweigh the costs or don't impact key strategic priorities, then the incentives will be too weak. One or both companies won't have a good reason to put in the needed work, and the partnership won't last long.

▶ **Unbalanced incentives:** If one partner benefits far more than the other, the partnership will likely fail or become more of a supplier relationship. Remember those group projects in school where you did all the work but everyone got the same grade? Yeah, those weren't fun, and they're not fun in partnerships either.

▶ **Vague incentives:** Sometimes the incentives are there, but if you can't quantify them, it doesn't matter. If you can't measure the success, then it's hard to know whether both parties are truly benefiting.

#3: CULTURE OR BRAND VALUE MISMATCH

Culture and brand value match is important. These things influence the way teams work together, and that is crucial to execution. If the teams have different values and work differently, it will be hard to make progress. As a broad example, say that one team values creative collaboration while the other values self-sufficiency. You can imagine how those teams could get frustrated working together.

#4: LACK OF EXECUTIVE SUPPORT AND ALIGNMENT (AT ONE OR BOTH COMPANIES)

Partnerships are typically driven by business development

teams. However, these teams can't make a partnership happen alone. They need executive support. Strategic partnerships require time and resources, often from multiple departments. They also sometimes require significant changes in how a business is operated. Without executive alignment, it is often hard to get the needed buy-in from across departments within companies to make change happen.

Each company's partnership team should have an executive champion, someone from the C-suite. Executive champions for each company should ideally be at the same seniority level to ensure a balanced relationship with similar decision-making responsibilities.

#5: UNCLEAR ACCOUNTABILITY

In partnerships, it's best for BD to do the upfront work of establishing the partnership and then pass the reins for the actual execution of the partnership. Too often, though, one of two things happens due to unclear accountability:

▸ **BD keeps managing the partnership after the term sheet and contract are completed.** This may not go well. It's not typical that BD manages the partnership itself because the execution is usually driven by other departments depending on the scope of the partnering idea.

▸ **No one manages the execution at all.** This is even worse. Often businesses will dismiss a partnership as a bad deal because they don't hit the desired metrics. In reality, it may not have been a bad deal at all. There just wasn't anyone leading the execution of the work.

You should be thoughtful about the transition of managing the partnership, ensuring there's a clear leader assigned and accountable to drive the execution.

#6: POOR COMMUNICATION

A partnership is a huge organizational feat. Not only do partnerships usually require internal, cross-departmental coordination, they also require external, cross-*company* coordination. Communication is critical.

One of the biggest consequences of poor communication is misaligned priorities. If your priorities are misaligned, you and your partner won't be in sync. While you're working on task A, your partner will be working on task B, and you'll both be upset with the other for working on the "wrong" thing. Misaligned priorities create friction and disagreements in many areas: expectations for what is happening when, goals and objectives, and success metrics.

#7: LACK OF TRUST AND TRANSPARENCY

Trust is what turns a business relationship into a true partnership. With trust, you and your partner are on the same side. Without it, the partnership can feel more like you're rivals, vying to make sure you don't get the short end of the stick.

Lack of trust often becomes a problem when there are changes in the partner team. If the main partner contact leaves the company, it's often difficult for the partnership to continue because so much of the trust in the relationship was built off of that individual. So be prepared to not just build trust, but *rebuild* trust as needed. Predictability and consistency combined with transparency build credibility.

#8: LACK OF COMMITMENT TO THE LONG TERM

Sometimes, partnerships end. That's okay. An ending is only a failure if you're not prepared for it.

Consider the partnership between Twitter and DataSift, a third-party data reseller. Twitter decided to build their own business to sell data directly instead of through DataSift, ending the partnership and turning the two companies into competitors. In many cases, this type of move could be devastating to a smaller company's future, but DataSift seemed to have planned for this potential scenario. DataSift was not reliant on Twitter data, and they had engagements with other companies in case any of their relationships shifted.

In a partnership, you can't control your partner's business or whether they become a competitor, but you *can* plan scenarios and reduce your company's risk with a contingency plan. In some scenarios, you may want to avoid being too reliant on one partnership, which can become tricky if not proactively managed. However, there are also scenarios where the risk is worth it. If your prospect is making a strategic bet and you are too, a single-source commitment can yield much-better and more-strategic results over the long term than hedging bets across many various alternatives. Also, don't be afraid to work with the giants—they can change your company in extremely positive ways. But pay attention to how they've previously partnered and learn from others in the market area around you, so you can create an effective partnership approach.

Business strategies can duck and weave, so no matter what, get prepared. Build out how various scenarios might play out, so you and your company are not surprised and can stay ahead of your partnership journey.

Now that you know what *not* to do, let's talk about a better partnering approach for success: the Co-Elevate Method.

THE CO-ELEVATE METHOD

When I was a kid, my parents had a record player, and I loved to flip through their stack of vinyl LP records. That was how I first discovered what would become one of my favorite bands of all time. One day I pulled out a record album, and from the second I put it on, I was glued to my seat. I was surprised by all the different sounds and songs that this one band had created. Who the heck were these guys, and how had they managed to produce such an incredible range of music?

That album was *Sgt. Pepper's Lonely Hearts Club Band*, and the band was the Beatles, and the reason they were able to produce so many interesting, varied songs is simple: partnership. All four band members contributed to what made the Beatles so special. In particular, John Lennon and Paul McCartney stand out as the pair that did most of the songwriting and singing. Their styles were really different. Lennon songs tended to be dreamy and thought-provoking, while McCartney songs were more up-tempo and sentimental. They wrote great songs individually, but when they worked together and collaborated on a piece, it was absolute magic to me. ("A Day in the Life" is a masterpiece!)

So what do the Beatles have to do with company-to-company partnerships? Like the members of the Beatles tapping into multiple genres and styles, business partnerships enable the respective companies to create something magical. The Co-Elevate Method is founded on this simple, powerful idea: by working together, both partners can rise higher than they could alone.

The impacts of partnership can be far greater than you realize. Imagine for a moment that Lennon and McCartney never met and the Beatles never existed. We definitely wouldn't have "A Day in the Life," but what about Lennon's "Imagine" or McCartney's "Yesterday"? Personally, I don't think we'd have those songs either. Though solo written, they were really only possible because of the influence and experience from the Beatles.

The fact partnerships can be so powerful is exactly why it's so important to have a solid process for how to do them successfully. That's what the Co-Elevate Method is. It's a process I've used countless times and optimized to yield positive results time and time again. So let's unpack the core principles of the Co-Elevate Method. (You may notice that these principles connect back to several of the common pitfalls—that's by design, not coincidence.)

#1: WIN-WIN STRATEGY: YIN AND YANG

The number one most important characteristic of the Co-Elevate Method is that the partnership is win-win. A win-win partnership is where both parties see and feel that there is a strong benefit to participating in the partnership. It's not a win-lose scenario, where one party benefits at the expense (time, energy, money) of the other. A win-win partnership is the foundation for building mutual trust, respect, and value over time.

The key to a win-win partnership scenario is to find mutual value from both parties, no matter how big or small each company is, how long they've been in business, how many employees they have, or how much revenue they make. It's about identifying independent complementary factors that may seem opposite or contrary. I like to compare this balanced partnering mindset to the yin and yang concept. The yin and yang symbol is an excellent representation of partnerships because it shows the equality and unification needed to create something neither party could create alone:

In ancient Chinese philosophy, yin and yang is a concept of dualism, describing how seemingly opposite or contrary forces may actually be complementary, interconnected, and interdependent in the natural world. Well, of course the yin and yang concept has very deep roots, much deeper than I know of, but in the world of business and partnerships, it basically means finding partners where you can use each other's strengths to offset each other's weaknesses. The goal is to find the equal value equation: what's your win, what's my win.

In any partnership, a good place to start is what makes your business tick and what makes your prospect's business tick, and from that foundation, you design the partnership.

#2: BETTER TOGETHER: THE X FACTOR

When you build a win-win partnership, you often find that 1 + 1 = 3 (or more), basically stating, "The whole is greater than the sum of its parts."

This statement is usually attributed to Aristotle, though he didn't say it exactly like this. In his work *Metaphysics*, believed to have been written around 350 BC, he said, "In all things which have a plurality of parts, and which are not a total aggregate but a whole of some sort distinct from the parts, there is some cause." The modern shorter version is much easier to understand! But let's further dissect Aristotle's quote—he refers to a unified entity that is composed of distinct elements, but when combined, new characteristics are created from the interaction of the parts.

To relate this back to partnerships in business, putting two companies together is not enough to create a whole greater than the sum of its parts. For a 1 + 1 = 3 (or more) partnership, you need something more, "some cause." I call this the *X factor*.

The X factor is something created by the partnership that does not otherwise exist. The X factor could be any number of things: a new product, a new audience that neither company could reach alone, a new distribution channel, a new Idea or innovation that results from bringing talent together. The X factor can be difficult to define, but you know it when you see it.

For example, I once worked on a partnership with a photo-first social media platform. The platform was a great place to be inspired—from kitchen remodels to fashion styles—but it wasn't a great place to find and purchase the products that it showed. Though the platform had a predictable and mature advertising business, there was some market speculation around long-term monetization plans and revenue. Meanwhile, on third-party shopping websites, it could be difficult for customers to find what they were looking for because of the sheer volume of products.

Cue a partnership between the social media platform and online retailers in which they connected the platform's photos with links to where customers could actually buy the item. By working together, these companies solved each other's problems. The social media platform evolved from a place to browse to a place to shop, opening up online monetization plans. Simultaneously, online retailers improved their customer experience, because it was now easier for customers to find what they were looking for on the social media platform. The partnership reimagined and delivered a complete customer journey from inspiration through completing a purchase. That was the X factor that made the partnership greater than the sum of its parts.

#3: OPTIMISTIC REALISM

We're all human and work and act based on a mix of emotions and facts. Optimists gravitate to seeing the positive side of an idea or situation, while pessimists tend to focus on the downsides. Realists can see the facts without emotion and focus on the practicality, sometimes becoming overly logical. In partnerships, if you're too pessimistic, you'll never get an idea off the ground, but if you're too optimistic, you'll overlook important challenges, and if you're too realistic, you'll struggle with the emotional, relationship-building, and storytelling aspects of partnerships.

The solution is *optimistic realism*. Embrace the power of positive thinking combined with the objective lens of being rational.

This way you can come up with partnership ideas that are big and impactful but also achievable. Don't shy away from being a pessimist when you need to be, though. You need to poke holes in your own partnership ideas to ensure you know the drawbacks and risks. Basically, try to default to optimistic realism, but also ask yourself, "What does this situation call for?" If you're trying to get people excited about your ideas, more optimism may be needed. If you're trying to pressure-test your ideas or hash out negotiation terms, more realism and even pessimism can be helpful.

#4: IMPACT ON PRIORITIES

Every partnership should come with a business model of strong, balanced, measurable incentives:

▸ **Strong:** Does the partnership directly impact current or emerging strategic priorities? Do the benefits outweigh the costs?

▸ **Balanced:** Does each party have equal skin in the game? Are they getting a similar level of value?

▸ **Measurable:** Can the impact be tracked and measured?

For example, if your prospective partner is going to bring your product to their customers, then in return you could offer a strong revenue-sharing business model. Or maybe being able to offer your product would be a strong differentiator for your partner that helps them stand out above their competitors, allowing them to sell more of their own products or services.

Consider the partnership that Uber and Spotify formed in which Spotify users with premium accounts would be able to stream their own playlists on Uber rides. This partnership had a strong impact for both companies. It gave Uber a competitive advantage over other ride-sharing apps, encouraging riders to use Uber more and increasing rider loyalty. Spotify, meanwhile, was able to tap into Uber's user base in order to increase subscriptions to Spotify Premium. Key metrics for each company were impacted in a strong, balanced, and measurable way.

#5: SHARED PURPOSE AND COMPATIBLE CULTURES AND VALUES

With the Co-Elevate Method, it's like you're creating not just a partnership but an entirely new virtual company, with its own objectives, initiatives, and team. A shared purpose and compatible cultures and values help to hold that partnership company together. While business attributes and characteristics need to be different to balance each other out (that's the yin and yang), partnerships can be more successful when the companies' cultures and values are similar.

If culture or values don't match upfront, don't worry. This is not necessarily a showstopper. Cultures and values can be complementary even if they're not exactly the same—the difference can even be a strength. However, you do need to be aware of the mismatch and proactive in communication to prevent friction and potential issues, and you should at least have *some* shared values and culture.

Even if cultures and values are different, purpose—the *why* of the partnership—needs to be shared. Now, not *all* motivations for the partnership need to be shared. Either company might have its own confidential reasons for pursuing the partnership, but it's still important to have a shared vision both companies can align with.

For example, Apple and Nike have a long history of partnering together. Back in 2006 they partnered together on the Nike+iPod activity tracker. More recently, they partnered on the Apple Watch Nike, with custom app connectivity and exclusive straps. The partnership may work so well together in part because they have compatible and complementary company visions. Nike's vision statement is "to bring inspiration and innovation to every athlete in the world." Apple's mission is "to bring the best user experience to its customers through its innovative hardware, software, and services."

What's common between Nike and Apple? Innovation and a commitment to their customers. As former Nike CEO Mark Parker said when they released the Nike+iPod, "Nike+iPod is a partnership between two iconic, global brands with a shared passion for creating meaningful consumer product experiences through design and innovation." A powerful shared vision like that can lead to impactful partnership outcomes.

#6: OPERATIONAL RIGOR

Partnerships are rarely black and white. When you're working in the gray area, operational rigor becomes even more important. Approaching partnerships with a clear process of operational rigor is what prevents issues with leadership, communication, trust, and lack of contingency plans.

Operational rigor begins with understanding the next stages of the Co-Elevate Method (which correspond to the next four parts of the book):

▸ **Stage 1, Explore—The Big Idea:** This stage is about assessing the strengths, weaknesses, and needs of your company; coming up with the Big Idea for the partnership; and identifying potential partners.

▸ **Stage 2, Align—Taking Flight:** In this stage, you start "selling" your Big Idea, pitching both internally to gain support and externally to potential partners in order to reach alignment and sign a partnership deal.

▸ **Stage 3, Execute—Gaining Altitude:** This stage is the nilly-gritty work of the partnership itself, in which you create and follow a shared work plan, establish a meeting cadence, and so on.

▶ **Stage 4, Grow—Reaching New Heights:** After you have an initial partnership under your belt, you can begin expanding existing partnerships and creating your own unique partnering recipe.

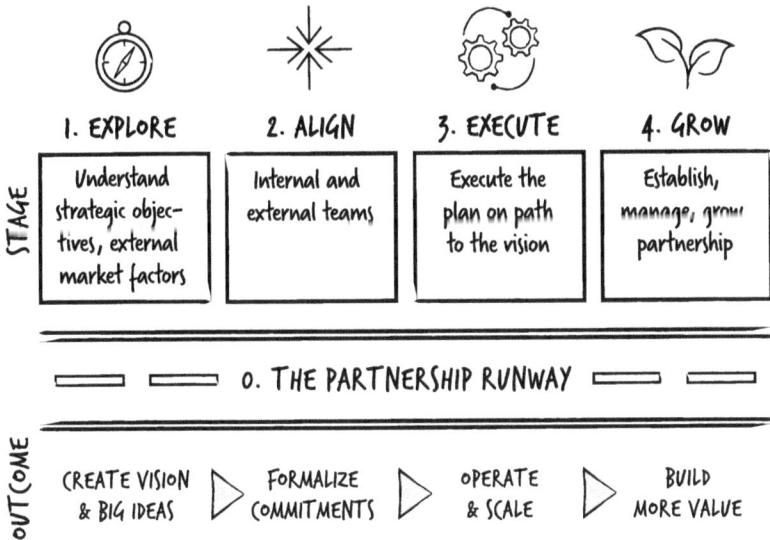

	1. EXPLORE	2. ALIGN	3. EXECUTE	4. GROW
STAGE	Understand strategic objectives, external market factors	Internal and external teams	Execute the plan on path to the vision	Establish, manage, grow partnership

0. THE PARTNERSHIP RUNWAY

OUTCOME	CREATE VISION & BIG IDEAS	FORMALIZE COMMITMENTS	OPERATE & SCALE	BUILD MORE VALUE

Managing partnerships is a unique challenge because you're not just managing internal teams but external ones too. For a partnership to succeed, you will need strong leadership, a shared work plan, an established meeting cadence, and a whole lot of communication and documentation. Entire books could be (and have been) written about program management. Since this particular book is about partnerships and not program management, I've focused more on the first two stages and how to establish successful partnerships as opposed to the nitty-gritty work of managing existing partnerships. But don't worry—I'll still share plenty of tips and best practices to help you in managing each stage of the partnership with operational rigor.

PARTNERING JUJUTSU

One of my technical colleagues refers to my partnering work as "jujutsu." It's a good description. *Jujutsu* can be translated as "yielding-art." The core philosophy of the jujutsu martial art is to shift the opponent's force rather than exerting one's own force. Likewise, in partnerships, while there's no opponent, it's a delicate dance. The Co-Elevate Method is all about alignment and building value versus only pushing for what your company wants.

In the next chapter, I'll go through a quick primer about how to establish BD and partnerships as a discipline in your company, including hiring and team structure. If you're a BD veteran and believe you have the right team in place, feel free to skip ahead.

CHAPTER 3

BUILDING PARTNERSHIPS AS A DISCIPLINE

This chapter is meant to help you level set and understand the function of partnerships and business development at a practical level within your company. Partnering is an often-misunderstood discipline as it is a triangulation of several skill sets with varying specializations based on the type of partnerships you're pursuing and where you're at in the BD process. I hope to help you formalize the partnering role within your company to limit ambiguity, prevent overlap, and clarify responsibilities.

First, you may have noticed that I use the terms *BD* and *partnerships* fairly interchangeably. Does that mean BD is the same as partnerships? No! Business development is a set of activities to help grow a business beyond the current set of activities that the company may be engaged in—a.k.a., you're developing the business. Partnerships are a strategy within BD to help grow the business. BD identifies and creates opportunities for growth. Partnerships are the primary manifestation of how BD activities are put into action to achieve results and outcomes. For the purposes of this book, I'll continue to use the terms somewhat interchangeably since we're focusing on the role of partnerships in BD specifically.

While BD and partnerships are not the same thing, they are deeply connected to one another, so it's worth diving deeper into how BD functions.

WHAT IS BUSINESS DEVELOPMENT? A FANCY WAY OF SAYING "SALES"?

The first thing to understand is that business development is not sales, and sales is not business development. The two often get put in the same bucket because they are both outward-facing roles that engage externally and are designed to drive growth. Plus, BD can be ill defined within an organization, while sales is well defined and structured, so BD is often put in the same teams as sales and held to the same metrics. However, they are two essential yet different functions in a business, with different but related goals and processes.

For example, BD's goal may be to grow core company metrics, some of which may not be revenue oriented (e.g., reducing costs, increasing customer satisfaction, becoming more sustainable in operations, increasing speed to market with new innovations, etc.). For sales, the primary goal is to increase revenue through sales to customers. The BD and sales engagement processes and business models may also differ. For example, BD engagement processes are often bespoke and customized, because every partner and project may be different, while sales engagements may be more similar from customer to customer, as the base product offering is often the same. Now, there can be more similarities than differences between BD and sales depending on the organization or product offerings. Techniques such as *consultative selling* have common approaches to BD processes with a focus on building relationships with companies by understanding their needs and providing tailored solutions. Conversation is focused on company challenges and goals, rather than prioritizing product features. Compensation for BD and sales roles is usually different as well, and compensation structure drives actions and priorities. Typically, sales leaders are compensated with less base pay and performance-based pay tied to their sales quotas, while BD leaders have higher base pay and may have performance bonuses tied to BD milestones, like contracts and growth outcomes, but no quotas. When BD and Sales teams work together engaging with the same partner or customers, the key is to first align internally on common goals and outcomes to help one another reach those objectives.

For the most part, because of these characteristics, when building strategic partnerships, you want to engage with a BD or partnerships team, since their goals and ways of operating may better align with building a strategic partnership, leading to a higher probability of success.

WHEN SHOULD YOU HIRE BD?

Remember the story from the introduction? I was working at an early-stage tech start-up, and right when it seemed like everything was going to fall apart, a strategic partnership turned everything around. Ultimately, it was a success story about partnering, but it didn't start that way.

I had never been at a start-up so early before. The company didn't have a product in-market yet, and there were fewer than twenty employees, most of whom I knew from my previous role at a Fortune 500 company. I really had to get scrappy and build the partnering function from the ground up. I got to work developing new go-to-market strategies for the company with the CEO and even started exploring new product ideas that partners could amplify through their sales channels. I was generating interest, which was my job. But I was also causing distraction. The product and engineering teams wanted to focus on the core product, and I was creating opportunities that pulled their attention away into developing demos and prototypes for partner meetings, which was impacting the overall timeline for our general launch.

Everything worked out in the long run, but with the benefit of hindsight, if I could go back and do it again, I think I should have been a consultant to start, as the company simply wasn't ready for a full BD function.

Knowing when to hire BD can be tricky. Joining a company in the very early stages can be a risk for any function but particularly BD. When BD happens too early, it can be destructive or, less dramatic, a distractor. At the same time, since there hasn't been a solid playbook for how BD should be organized, many companies embed the BD function as an afterthought, which can lead to inefficiencies and lost opportunities. Essentially: don't hire BD too early ... and don't hire BD too late.

So how do you know when you're ready? A BD person's job is to develop new opportunities for distribution and expansion (depending on the company objectives), so a good rule of thumb is that before you hire BD, you need to develop the first version of your product: an MVP, or minimum viable product. In some cases, in the very early stages of a company or business unit forming, BD can help with partnerships for tools and platforms. However, BD should not be drumming up new business or distribution opportunities without a clear product definition. Now, if there is a clear product definition and the launch date is committed to and not at risk, pre-launch BD efforts can be effective to plant seeds for valuable relationships prior to launch or soon thereafter. Pre-launch BD is also helpful if a partner or set of partners is needed to be part of the MVP.

Beyond this core prerequisite, here's a good checklist to know when you're ready to hire a BD role:

▸ Your business model and business rely on partnerships to launch your product.

▸ You'll soon be launching your product or have recently launched your product, and you need a point of contact for developing a distribution and user acquisition strategy beyond marketing and sales.

▸ Your company is being inundated with partnership requests, and many of those requests could be meaningful to the growth of your business.

If you're here reading this book, there's a good chance you're ready for BD, though exactly what that looks like can vary. If you've reached a point where you're ready to scale and grow in a big way, you will likely want a strong BD function within your company. If you're still in the earlier stages, where BD could be valuable but you don't have the resources (whether that's time, money, or talent) to support a full BD function, you might consider third-party consultants instead, so you can get the benefits of BD without as much commitment and investment.

WHAT SHOULD YOU LOOK FOR WHEN HIRING BD?

BD mindsets typically fall into two categories:

▸ **Builders:** BD builders create, or "build," the BD function. They essentially fly the BD plane while simultaneously building the plane and figuring out where to fly to. Builders are essential when a BD or partnering function is new or nonexistent in a company. They're leaders who help plan and set the direction of the company or initiative. They typically have a visionary mindset, focusing on strategy and the big picture. They're more likely to take risks, with the potential for higher rewards, and they learn from experience and experimentation. (E.g., "Let's refine BD's goals and metrics after we go do a few partnerships.")

▸ **Operators:** BD operators work within a framework and deliver consistent results quarter after quarter and year after year. They are crucial for maintaining the BD or partnering function. They're captains who are given a map and help the company navigate from point A to point B. They tend to have a management/operational mindset, with a focus on tactics and day-to-day execution. They value consistency and reliability over high-risk, high-reward approaches, and they follow established guidelines and processes. (E.g., "What are our goals and metrics as a department? What do we need to do to meet those?")

Now, don't think about these mindsets as two distinct people. A single individual can possess traits from both mindsets. Both builders and operators are crucial to a company's success, and the most productive and impactful BD individuals are able to combine these BD mindsets into one.

Experience plays a role here. If you're a CEO looking to build a BD function from zero, you'll want someone with a proven track record, because there's a lot of risk involved. Along similar lines, if you're a less experienced BD professional or you're new to partnering, I recommend you target roles in companies where more than 25 percent of the company's overall revenue is currently coming from BD and partnering. There's less risk when you're joining or inheriting an already working partnering function where the value of partnerships is recognized. It's totally okay if those initial partnerships were created and are being managed by the CEO or the sales team or even the product or marketing teams. In fact, that's a good thing, since you then know the company or initiative really needs you.

Now, anyone can try to create a partnership, right? Yes! But can they do it successfully and make game-changing impact? Maybe. Even within BD, not everyone will be great at partnerships. BD professionals come from many walks of life and backgrounds, and BD and partnering require different and shared skill sets based on the partnership idea. BD managers don't always make great partnership managers and vice versa.

Hiring a BD generalist when a partnering specialist is needed can work, but the skills gap needs to be addressed upfront by adding someone with partnering as a strength to the partnership core team. Likewise, hiring a partnering specialist may limit your ability to expand and grow into new market segments, but with the right training, a specialist can elevate to a generalist with the ability to operate closer to the CEO, influencing company strategy and direction.

Sometimes you can strike gold with a BD "athlete" that can do both BD and partnering. A BD athlete, as I define it, is a person who possesses a wide range of BD skills from relationship building to dealmaking to strategic partnership development. Not only can a BD athlete be effective across different parts of the partnership life cycle, but they also can develop effective business strategies across a wide range of market segments and vertical areas. Depending on the company and initiative objectives, role or market segment specialization may be needed, but keep in mind that strategic plans change and markets also do, so if you have the time and talent pool available, look for a BD athlete. If you are the BD professional reading this, the goal of this book is to make you a BD athlete, and if you believe you already are, let's make you even more indispensable to your company.

If you want a BD athlete who can operate and deliver at super-high levels, you need someone with a balance of role discipline expertise and industry domain expertise.

Discipline expertise is all the knowledge and skills related to BD and partnering. These skills are transferable across partnerships, businesses, and industries. Be aware that since there are not many standard processes in BD and partnering, many BD professionals will have developed their own processes to achieve the outcomes that are important to their companies.

In addition to discipline expertise, some initiatives will require domain or subject matter expertise in a certain industry or set of industries. If your desired partnering idea requires deeply integrating your product or services with existing companies in a specific domain, knowing how to navigate that market area can be crucial. Understanding how the related ecosystem works, from the supply chain to go-to-market, can make the partnerships more effective and likely to succeed. Additionally, if BD professionals have domain expertise, they may already have relationships with relevant contacts and companies, so they can hit the ground running.

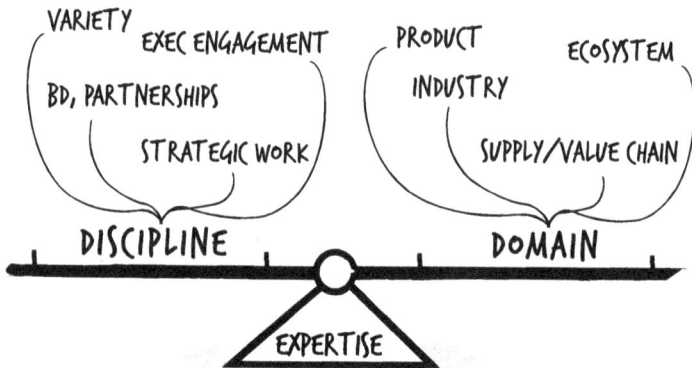

Once you've started hiring for BD, the next big choice is how to structure the function.

WHAT TO LOOK FOR IN A PARTNERING CONSULTANT

In my experience, partnering usually ends up becoming such a core role that you will want to hire for it internally. Still, there are times when a consultant makes more sense. Good BD and partnering consultants can be difficult to find. Part of this is simply because while partnering is a time-proven strategy, the partnering function is still relatively ambiguous. So finding *any* partnering-specific consultant can be challenging. Often what you'll find instead is "strategy consultants." Regardless of the consultant's title, look for these traits to increase the chances of a successful, valuable relationship:

▸ **Proven experience with partnerships:** Have they successfully created partnerships at other companies? Do they have experience in your particular industry or with companies that have a similar profile to yours (in terms of size, product/service, etc.)?

▸ **An understanding of your company:** Partnerships should be directly linked to the company's core objectives and key metrics. Any good partnering consultant will want to first come in and really understand your business before they start developing partnership ideas and a list of potential partners to pursue.

▸ **A predictable method:** The consultant should have a partnering method or process of some kind. You don't want someone who is just winging it.

HOW SHOULD YOU STRUCTURE THE TEAM?

There are two fundamental structures for BD and partnering functions: centralized or decentralized. Each approach has pros and cons. There is also a hybrid structure that can be customized to your broader organizational setup.

Centralized means there is a BD and partnerships team that acts as a resource to various internal organizations. Centralized BD teams understand the BD discipline and often have goals that are aligned with the success of the overall BD function combined with aligned goals with the specific business unit that the BD role is supporting. Typically, centralized BD has a leader that directly reports to the CEO or CBO (Chief Business Officer). The big pro of this structure is that BD is closely tied to the broad goals of the company, with a strong alignment between the partnering strategy and corporate strategy. This drives them to create partnerships with a big impact for the company. The con is that the function may lack some domain expertise. There's also the potential for disconnect between BD and the internal team they're supporting—for example, while working with the product team, BD might come in with their own set of goals and metrics while the product team has a different set of objectives. This could lead to friction, with BD being seen as "outsiders."

A decentralized model allows the BD role to be fully embedded in a particular business unit and engaged with cross-functional team members day-to-day. The goals and objectives for the BD role are aligned to the success of the business unit and related product initiative. In the decentralized structure, depending on the size and maturity of the operation, the BD role reports into the head of the business unit, not a BD executive who reports to the CEO or CBO. The pro is that with BD fully embedded, they typically have more domain expertise in the market the business unit operates within. They will understand the dynamics of that particular business unit and space, and they will be closely aligned with the business unit's goals. The con is that they may be less connected to the company's broader strategy, leading to partnerships that, even if successful, do not move the needle in a meaningful way for the company as a whole.

Personally, my preference is for centralized BD, because I think it's important for BD and partnering to be closely tied to the corporate strategy. Decentralized BD can be useful, though, especially when there are very distinct products. For example, Yamaha sells both musical products and motorcycles. Finding one person who can navigate both those industries could be challenging, so having a decentralized BD team where one person specializes in the music space and one in the motorcycle space could be smart. Likewise, if you're operating in different regions or countries—say, the United States and Japan—decentralized BD might be the right choice so you can better understand the preferences and needs of those consumers.

Often, I'll see a hybrid of centralized and decentralized BD, where there is a centralized BD team that reports to the CEO but certain members of that team are embedded (or dotted line) into key business units.

Ultimately, how you structure BD and partnering should be based on the culture of your company, particularly how decisions are made and the core principles of how employees work together. The right structure will evolve with the company, so just put something into place as a pilot test, and if you see it's not working, change it!

Once you've chosen your structure, you then need to decide where the BD function should live within the company. Who will BD report to? There are a few common approaches, some more effective than others:

▶ **The head of an established department, like sales, marketing, or corporate development/strategy:** Sometimes companies don't want to make BD its own department and instead place the function under an existing department. The most common approach is to make BD part of sales, but I do not recommend this, as it will prevent the BD function from maximizing its potential. Remember: sales and BD goals and metrics may be different. Thus the actions and activities are different too. BD is closer to marketing than sales, where BD (in its simplest form) amplifies a company's product or service through partner channels to increase customer reach or brand. But again, this needlessly limits BD's potential. If you want to place BD under an existing department, I recommend corporate development or corporate strategy, as those departments may have similar goals to BD.

- **Chief Operating Officer (COO):** I've also seen BD report into the COO, which can work effectively as a general partnering and BD function for the company. The big pro of this approach is that all licensing and partnerships for a company can be centralized and optimized versus having various business units doing their own deals for internal tools, working with various vendors, and so on. The con is the growth goals and new BD activities could be spread too thin. This doesn't mean you have to avoid this structure; you just need to look out for it. Ensure there is an aligned balance of priorities for the BD manager among all the things they are point on.

- **CEO:** Having a savvy, business-oriented CEO leading BD and partnering can be a huge asset if you're an early-stage company, as having top-to-top relationships can accelerate decision-making and deals between companies. The reality, though, is that this approach simply won't scale. Eventually, the CEO won't be able to do it all and will need someone else leading BD, even if that individual keeps reporting to the CEO. Additionally, BD professionals have specialized skills, so instead of trying to go at it alone, CEOs should engage a BD professional that they know and trust to get the BD function started.

▶ **Chief Business Officer (CBO) or Chief Revenue Officer (CRO):** In some companies, all general business functions report into a CBO or CRO, such as sales, BD, legal, finance, and other business-related functions and teams. This can work well because the CBO/CRO function provides a comprehensive perspective across the business and can make changes or optimizations for efficiency.

Depending on the maturity of your company and overall organization, there may be obvious functions where the BD team should be reporting into. For most businesses I recommend BD be its own department reporting into a C-suite executive.

WHAT'S YOUR BD STRATEGY?

In the next sections of the book, we'll be diving into lots of strategies for successful partnerships, but before that, you should have an idea of your overall BD strategy. In my opinion, every company should have the same basic BD strategy: become a partner of choice. You want to craft and maneuver your BD strategy to build a reputation as a trusted partner with proven win-win principles. While you may not be the best partner in all cases, external prospects will want to come to you first to explore partnership possibilities.

Over time, you can develop your company into the partner of choice by utilizing a blended push-and-pull strategy, which has two layers of meaning.

The first meaning is about your engagement approach with partner prospects. Do you go in with a sales approach in which you push the partnership idea to them? Or do you try to pull them into the concept, encouraging them to contribute to and take ownership of the partnership idea? Ideally, you will do a little bit of both, with more focus on the pull. If you just push, prioritizing only what your company wants, or you just pull, allowing other companies to drive the formation of the partnership, you won't be able to form a true, mutually beneficial Co-Elevate Partnership. You can think of this push and pull as the balancing act that leads to a win-win partnership.

The second layer of meaning is about how you come up with ideas. With a *push* strategy, you build an inventory of partnership ideas that resonate with your internal teams, and then you "push" those ideas to partner prospects. With a *pull* strategy, you start by assessing the market and understanding what prospects want. You identify the current demand for partnerships and then "pull" in those ideas and concepts to review and expand on with internal teams. If another company approaches you for a partnership, that also falls under "pull" BD. To simplify further, you can think of "push" as inside-out BD and "pull" as outside-in BD. Ideally, you will use a blended push-pull model to ensure you're meeting your internal needs (push) as well as responding to and leveraging the partner ecosystem demand (pull).

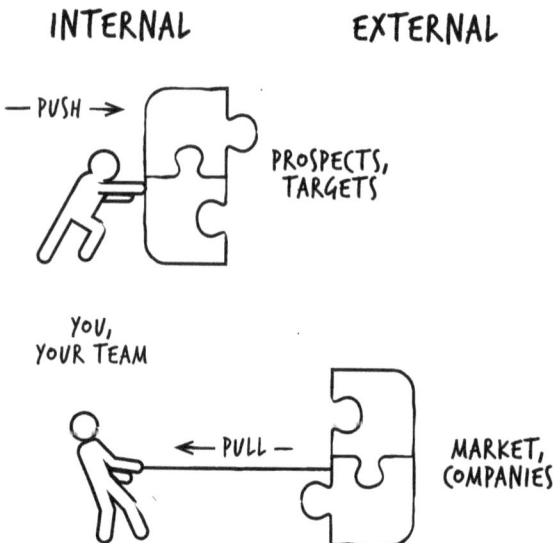

THE CREATIVE GROWTH ENGINE

BD is all about finding creative ways to grow a company or initiative. Effective BD can help your company not only increase customers and revenue, but also improve your brand recognition, customer satisfaction, product offerings, and more. If the BD function is consciously designed instead of being an afterthought, partnerships will run more smoothly.

Now that we've covered how to set up and hire the team, let's look at the common partnership types and models you might encounter and use.

CHAPTER 4

THE WIDE WORLD OF PARTNERSHIPS

Partnerships come in every flavor, shape, and size under the sun. Using the Co-Elevate Method, each strategic partnership you build will be unique. However, there are some patterns and partnership models you can draw from as a foundation.

First, partnerships often fall into three main categories, which can be stand-alone or combined. There are several other ways to partner, but we'll start with these categories:

▶ **Marketing:** using your company's or another company's brand in a variety of ways

▶ **Product:** integrating your company's or another company's technology on the product and user experience level

▶ **Distribution:** using the distribution network of your company or another company to grow a user base/audience

Marketing partnerships are a good idea if amplifying your brand is important to you. They allow you to tap into the *halo effect*, which is a cognitive bias where our positive impressions of one thing positively influence our impressions of an associated thing. Basically, if you partner with a strong brand, they cast a "halo" over your brand by association, boosting your brand. It's key that you and your team are honest about the value of your brand. Don't kid yourself! You may love your company brand, but does it resonate with the target audience? Do your target customers know your brand, and does it help to engage them? Are you known as a market leader, or are there others that have a stronger brand in your market segment? If you opt for a marketing partnership, it can take many forms. The brands can be on equal footing (see "The Co-Brand"), or one brand can lead and the other follow (see "The 'Powered By' or Ingredient Brand"). In some cases, only one of the brands is shown to customers even though the product or service is built and operated by another company (see "White Label and Rebadging").

Product partnerships are smart if you want to expand your product or offering. You may find it faster and simpler to work with other companies to fill the gap in your offerings versus building everything yourselves. Conversely, you may have a strong product, service, or technology that could fill the gap for others. The previously discussed Apple Watch Nike is a great example of two companies coming together for a product partnership.

If your big goal is to reach additional customers, distribution partnerships can be worth exploring. Using another company's go-to-market sales engine can amplify your sales and open up new market areas for you. Or you can serve as the go-to-market sales engine for another company's product or service and get a cut of the proceeds. Distribution partnerships can be especially powerful when you're trying to break into a new segment, whether that be industry, country, region, or so on.

Marketing, product, and distribution partnerships can each take shape in various forms, and often partnerships will span more than one category. For example, say two companies join forces to create a new product together. Chances are they may also end up using each other's brands and distribution networks as they market and sell that product to customers. Also remember that a Co-Elevate Partnership is a two-way street, with both parties benefiting.

So now let's look at some specific partnership models. This list is *far* from exhaustive. It's a small sample of the partnership models I see most often. Additionally, each model should be viewed as a framework that you can customize to your needs as opposed to a ready-to-go, "plug-and-play" prototype. Again, partnerships are rarely one-dimensional. They tend to span multiple models. We'll talk about this later, but the more ways you can use a partnership across your company, the better. So use these partnership models to expand your ideas, not limit them.

THE CO-BRAND

A co-brand is when two brands are looking to bring a joint product to customers. This is different from a sponsorship or a promotion, which can be used to amplify a product partnership or a strategic marketing relationship. A true co-brand is a mutually beneficial alliance where the equity or key product attribute of two brands is combined to create a new product or service.

Co-branding can be an excellent way to grow a company without having to make a major investment in resources or create costly marketing campaigns. It creates a best-of-both-worlds relationship where each business benefits from the reputation, image, and customer base of the other. Co-branding can bring immediate recognition to product extensions and can create the ability to charge a premium price. If executed properly, co-branding can pay off greatly for all involved and make customers happy.

One of my favorite co-brand examples is not a new partnership but one that started in 1975—proof that partnerships have long been a viable business strategy. The co-brand was between the cosmetics company Bonne Belle and beverage company Dr. Pepper. In 1973, Bonne Belle launched the flavored lip balm line Lip Smacker. They started with familiar flavors, like strawberry. Two years later, with the line a success, they started exploring more flavors. Cue the co-brand partnership with Dr. Pepper, to create Dr. Pepper–flavored lip balm. It was a huge success, with the partnership standing the test of time through numerous fashion trends and styles. The Dr. Pepper Lip Smacker even found a renewed fame after going viral on TikTok. In 2022, the Dr. Pepper Lip Smacker was finally discontinued after nearly fifty years, but the Coca-Cola Lip Smacker sets with Sprite and Fanta flavors are alive and well.

While co-branding can lead to great results, it isn't a be-all and end-all solution and should be executed with caution. If co-branding initiatives aren't performed correctly, they can turn into blunders. The Target and Neiman Marcus story from chapter 2, "A Winning Partnering Method," is a clear example. The farther apart two brands are in terms of quality or perception, the more difficult a co-brand will be.

THE "POWERED BY" OR INGREDIENT BRAND

In a co-brand, the partners are fairly equal in coming together to create something new. In a "powered by" or ingredient brand, one partner takes the lead with the other providing some key ingredient to the lead partner's offering. As opposed to the two creating a unique product together, the host or lead brand is making use of the ingredient brand to provide a better product or service. Gore-Tex and 3M's Thinsulate are great examples, where one company licenses out their innovative technology to many other brands.

A landmark "powered by" brand was the "Intel Inside" initiative. For a long time, while Intel had a great reputation with manufacturers because of the quality of its chips, it was not well known by end consumers. The "Intel Inside" initiative helped change that. Intel (the ingredient brand) partnered with PC manufacturers (the host brands), who began to advertise the Intel chips that powered their products by adding the "Intel Inside" logo. Some people were skeptical about the campaign. Would customers actually care about the technical components inside of their computers? The answer ended up being a resounding yes. Intel was able to build a brand for itself among consumers, who learned to recognize Intel processors as a sign of quality. The host brands benefitted as well, being able to use Intel's new quality brand in their own products. Still today, we see the influence of this initiative. When you go shopping for a laptop, you'll often find a sticker indicating what chip is inside, or the processor will be one of the first pieces of information given in the item's description.

Often, a host brand and an ingredient brand are both trying to build their business and brand. Ingredient brands often sell to other companies as opposed to selling directly to consumers, so a "powered by" branding initiative is critical for them to build brand awareness with end consumers. That brand awareness can help them secure more partnerships and supplier relationships. For the host brand, the ability to associate their products with an existing brand that has recognition and reputation can be incredibly valuable.

The difficulty with this type of partnership is striking a balance so that not only one brand benefits from the partnership. Also, if the right brand balance is not identified early, this type of collaboration could dilute brand equity over time.

WHITE LABEL AND REBADGING

White labeling is the practice of applying a different badge or trademark to an existing product and marketing that variant as a distinct product. Essentially, the same product is sold under different brand names. In the automotive and consumer electronics industries, this practice is often referred to as *rebadging* or *badge engineering*. As an example, Toyota partnered with BMW to utilize the Z4 platform for the Toyota Supra. You'll also run into acronyms like ODM (original design manufacturer), which is a company that typically designs a product to be customized (to a certain extent) and branded by an OEM (original equipment manufacturer), which is a company that typically is the brand of the end product.

Due to the high cost of designing and engineering a new product or establishing a brand (which may take many years to gain acceptance), it's far less expensive to white label and rebadge a product once or multiple times than to create different models.

Have you heard the rumor that Costco's Kirkland Signature vodka is actually relabeled Grey Goose vodka? Well, I hate to disappoint you, but that's not true. However, the Kirkland Signature brand *is* a great example of white labeling. Kirkland Signature batteries? They're produced by Duracell. Costco's diapers? Produced by Kimberly-Clark, the maker of Huggies.

White labeling can also be applied to services, as with Shopify, which provides customizable online storefronts for many merchants. When you visit one of these websites, you may not even realize it's run by Shopify, because Shopify is in the background, letting the merchants' brands take center stage.

White labeling works for many companies, but keep in mind that product quality from the supplying partner could impact the lead brand reputation. Also, white label products are typically sold to multiple companies, making it difficult for a brand to differentiate itself from competitors, so think about possible value-added features or offerings.

PRODUCT INTEGRATION OR BUNDLING

Product partnerships often follow either an *integration* or a *bundling* model.

Let's say you want to sell your product (or service) to another company's existing audience. You have three main ways to do that:

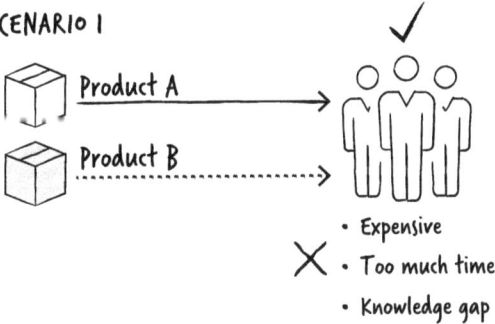

SCENARIO 1

Product A
Product B

- Expensive
- Too much time
- Knowledge gap

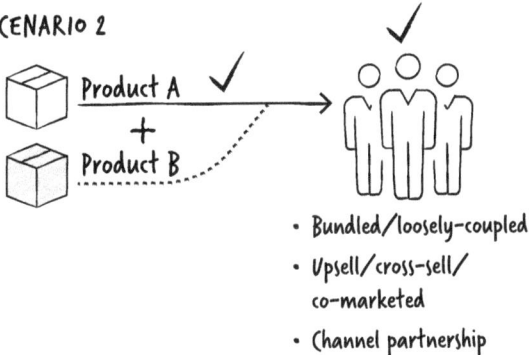

SCENARIO 2

Product A
+
Product B

- Bundled/loosely-coupled
- Upsell/cross-sell/ co-marketed
- Channel partnership

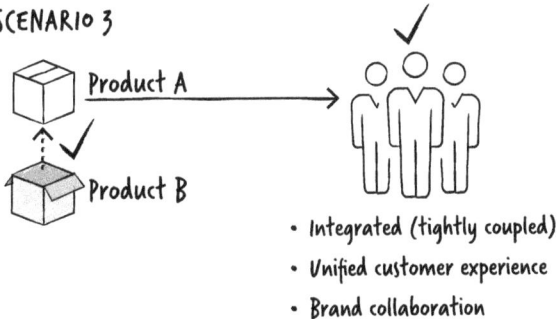

SCENARIO 3

Product A
Product B

- Integrated (tightly coupled)
- Unified customer experience
- Brand collaboration

In the first scenario, you are tapping into the existing audience, but you're basically going at it alone, which is expensive and requires more time to gain a foothold.

The second scenario is bundling. Your product is paired with the product that already exists. It could be part of an upsell or cross-sell. For example, if you make phone cases, you might form a partnership with a phone manufacturer in which your case is bundled at a discount with each new phone. Because your product is attached to the existing product, it's much easier to sell.

The third scenario is integration. The customer is not purchasing two separate products but a single product that contains components from both companies. This might be combined with a co-brand, the "powered by," or ingredient brand marketing partnership. In this scenario there is a unified customer experience, and your "product" is naturally sold, because it becomes part of the existing product.

THE TECHNOLOGY PARTNER

Partnerships are not only to grow your customer base or amplify your brand; with a technology partner, they can also be a catalyst for accelerating your product and technology roadmaps. Technology partnerships can provide access to adjacent technologies that enhance your own product through innovation and delivery of new features. A great example is Salesforce and DocuSign partnering to bring DocuSign's document operations into the Salesforce CRM (customer relationship management) platform, providing simplified workflows and processes all in one place.

Technology partnerships often cross multiple categories. For example, a technology partnership can lead to a new combined product offering. A great example is a streaming service partnering with consumer electronics companies to pre-integrate and get their streaming service on TVs, game consoles, and stream-

ing boxes. Tech partnerships can also cross into distribution partnerships, enabling new go-to-market channels for developers
and companies.

When done right, technology partnerships can be super effective, but these types of partnerships can be difficult to create and
manage since they take more product and engineering engagement. Because this partnership type requires a lot of time and
resources, it should be core to your business, meaning it's not a
nice-to-have that your company could live without; it's a must-have
that could make a transformational change for your company.

GO-TO-MARKET PARTNERSHIP

As discussed previously, sales is not BD, and BD is not sales,
but they have a lot in common and often cross paths. There are
some sales-oriented partnering models that can help with distribution and increase the mutual strategic value of the relationship beyond a transactional buyer-seller engagement into a go-
to-market partnership.

There are three basic ways to sell:

▶ **Sell-to:** This is a typical buy-sell sales model where one
company is selling into another company, so not necessarily partnering.

▶ **Sell-through:** This is when one company sells another
company's product or service. This is also known as a
resell or *reseller* motion. Depending on the arrange-
ment, either the reseller or the product/service company may be responsible the selling price. The reseller
incentive may be a percentage of the selling price or a
bounty payment for each sale. In many cases a reseller
may prepurchase a product/service at a discount rate
and then sell it at higher price to customers to generate
a profit. Value-added resellers (VARs) typically bundle

additional services based on the end customer's needs. Resellers are also referred to as *distributors* or *channel partners*, with channel partners focusing on a certain sales channel, like government or healthcare, where sales specializations may be required.

▸ **Sell-with:** This is when the sales teams from two companies join forces to convert prospects to buying customers. This is also known as a *co-sell* or *co-seller* motion. This type of motion requires sales teams to map out customers in segments (e.g., regional, industry, or other categories). When two companies come together to develop a joint product or service, there is a natural need for their respective sales teams to explore how best to work together. Referral partners and affiliate partners are subtypes of the sell-with motion. Referral partners send you potential customers in exchange for a commission for the ones that convert to paying customers, and affiliate partners are focused more on promoting your product or services to their audience, often for a sponsorship fee of some kind.

Sell-through and sell-with motions both have potential to form into partnerships. Moving from strictly sell-to to sell-through and sell-with gives you the opportunity to build your sales funnel and expand your go-to-market distribution, particularly when your sales team doesn't have needed contacts or existing relationships.

PLATFORM PARTNERSHIP

When you think of partnerships, you probably think about individuals or companies that can help you build innovative products or co-marketing campaigns, but there's another partner type you shouldn't discount: platforms.

I often see platform partnerships in the context of the "thousand flowers" concept, in which the platform provides developer tools, allowing seeds to be planted, and then sees which ideas bloom. As companies continue to scale up, they often start looking for ways to turn products or services into platforms. We've seen this occur over the last few decades in the technology space. First you build the core product (hardware) with the killer use cases (software) that prove that the core product is viable and can serve an unmet need. With the software layer being made up of applications (apps), a company can provide great ways for "partners" (developers) to create apps for their platform.

Simply using a platform is not the same as a platform partnership. Let's go back to the Shopify example. If you're a merchant using Shopify, that's a white labeling partnership, not a platform partnership. In contrast, PayPal partnering with Shopify to serve as the credit and debit card processor for Shopify Payments *is* a platform partnership. A platform partnership is a strategic relationship with the platform as a whole, in which you are integrated with, offered by, referred by, or in some way boosted by the platform.

If you are partnering with a platform, the big benefit is access to a wide audience, with a one-to-many distribution. By working with *one* platform, you actually end up working with *many* companies.

The challenge is platform providers typically don't want to work with you directly. They will say, "We have a suite of tools and a website where you can see how our APIs are set up for you. It's turnkey." When that happens, it's a sign you're not working with a BD or partnering contact but likely with a developer program manager. These managers are most interested in onboarding more developers to their platform, so you will be pushed to the same set of tools as others, and you'll compete on your own merits. Well, that's not a partnership!

Creating a true partnership with a platform can be challenging and takes work. Start by better understanding how to make the platform company more successful. Ask them questions like this, to understand their motivations and what makes them tick:

▶ What is the profile of the most successful developer on your platform?

▶ What were the metrics that defined their success?

▶ What new use cases do you think would be most interesting to your customers?

▶ How can we be the best partner for you and become your next success story?

If you can't have a live conversation with the platform company, look at the apps that have been developed on the platform and figure out which ones have been most successful. App store metrics are a good starting point. Also look at which developers have been highlighted on the platform's website or featured on stage at events or conferences. What characteristics does the platform company use to decide which developers to showcase?

If you're the platform, you can think about these same things in reverse. Which partnerships will help your platform attract more developers and end customers? How can you be the best partner for your ideal developers and help them be successful?

JOINT VENTURE

A joint venture is a type of strategic partnership in which the collaborating companies establish and jointly own and operate a legally independent and separate entity. For example, United Launch Alliance (ULA) is a fifty-fifty joint venture by Boeing and Lockheed Martin to reduce costs of launch services to the US government. The companies that are part of the joint venture typically have equal stake in the entity and share its expenses and revenue. A joint venture is developed from resources and assets provided by the involved parties. This could be a step toward acquisition consideration and due diligence for direct equity investment.

CO-OPETITION

Co-opetition is the act of cooperation between competing companies. An overall goal of co-opetition is to move a market from a zero-sum game, where a single winner takes all, to one where the end result benefits the whole and engages additional market participants and offers consumers more options.

For example, an online retailer of e-books and a consumer technology company were competitors, as they both produced e-readers. However, they established an agreement to allow the distribution of the retailer's e-books directly to the consumer technology company's tablets. Through co-opetition, the retailer gained a wider market, and the consumer technology company was able to provide a better experience to its customers, through more comprehensive content.

The co-opetition approach can lead to the expansion of the overall market and the formation of new business relationships or, in some cases, acquisitions. But be cautious with a partner in a co-opetition agreement. To be effective and sustainable, co-opetition requires upfront work to create mutual respect and trust between the partners, building loyalty and confidence. Simultaneously, you have to be careful to protect your company and brand. Based on a prospect's reputation and how they have operated with partners in the past, you can take on more or less risk.

PULLING IT ALL TOGETHER

Let's go through a final partnership example in this chapter: Red Bull and GoPro. The two have come together on Red Bull extreme sporting events, from mountain biking to skydiving. GoPro is the exclusive provider of point-of-view videos of these events. The two companies share the content rights on coproductions, and both distribute the content through their digital distribution networks. So what kind of partnership is this? All of them! Okay, I exaggerate, but there *are* a lot of components in this partnership. There are marketing aspects, something in between co-brand and "powered by." There's a product/technology aspect, where GoPro technology has been integrated into Red Bull events. And there's a distribution aspect, where both companies are "selling with" each other to distribute the content.

This is what a Co-Elevate Partnership can look like. It's not two companies coming together for a one-and-done initiative but a true strategic, long-term relationship that elevates both companies to a level they couldn't reach alone.

The runway is in place, so now it's time to dive into the Co-Elevate Method and start preparing for your first Co-Elevate Partnership. First up, stage 1, Explore—the Big Idea. While it's tempting to jump right into brainstorming ideas or potential partners, the best way to identify the right idea and prospect is to first understand your own needs. So we're going to start with a self-assessment.

STAGE 1

EXPLORE:
THE BIG IDEA

CHAPTER 5

WHAT'S THE GOAL, AND HOW WILL YOU GET THERE?

In 2018, I was working with a start-up e-scooter rental company. They had just launched their product a few months prior and had about ten thousand engaged users and growing. My job was to help develop a growth plan.

I thought partnering could be a part of the plan, so you might think I'd start with questions like: What partnerships would help the company? Who would be good partners? But those actually aren't the questions you should start with. There are more fundamental questions you have to answer first:

▶ What's our goal? Why?

▶ How do we measure success?

▶ What's our internal plan for growth?

▶ What are the company's strengths and weaknesses?

Partnerships are like a three-layer cake. Your first layer is a strategic business plan for your company. Then you can come up with a partnership strategy, the second layer. The third and final layer is creating a strategic partnership plan. Each one builds off of what comes before.

YOUR COMPANY STRATEGY

So the first step was figuring out the big goal, or "North Star." What are we trying to achieve? The CEO wanted to get to one million users.

From there, with an understanding of the metrics that measured business growth, my team and I could unpack the overall goal and define a path to get there. At the current growth rate, based on internal growth initiatives, it could take many years to reach that goal of one million users. We needed to think creatively to accelerate user growth, but we all felt a bit lost and overwhelmed. We didn't have the budget, the time, or the ideas for how to reach the ambitious objective. Many folks internally had different approaches to the problem, leading to misalignment on potential pathways for growth. I was in the middle of this misalignment. From our leadership to our working teams, we just could not agree on what to do next.

So I had to take the lead, outlining how as a company we would reach our goal. I needed a plan that was clear, concise, and convincing that would yield the right results. I knew what we were going after and why, so I next looked at our go-to-market strategy and considered the fundamental changes that needed to happen to scale user and business growth at a much faster rate. The majority of existing users were between the ages of eighteen and twenty-four, so we knew our offering was resonating well with this age group. Where are many eighteen- to-twenty-four-year-olds concentrated? College campuses! We created a program where universities would pay us a licensing fee and offer the product for free to students as a benefit. We first met with Harvard, MIT, and others in the Boston area, and those pilot universities opened up opportunities with the University of California system. A similar distribution model was then extended to corporate campuses, and the rest is history. By first deeply understanding our own company, we were able to design partnerships that made a real impact.

The root of building a partnership is truly understanding your company. Before you enter into a business partnership or even contemplate a partnership approach, do a thorough self-assessment of your company across product and technology assets (including IP), people and resource skill sets, and business and brand value. This is how you'll understand not only what to look for in a partner but also what you can offer in return. By starting with what makes your business tick, you ensure that the partnership ideas you develop later will actually move the right needles.

PARTNERING NORTH STAR

Throughout this chapter you'll be answering several important questions and doing some helpful exercises. To get the most value out of this self-assessment, write everything down in a Partnering North Star document.

At a minimum, this document should include:

▶ Company mission

▶ Key metrics

▶ Company SWOT analysis

▶ Partnering strategy

This document will help you stay motivated through the partnership process. If the end goal and desired outcome of a partnership is not clear, it will feel like you're on a treadmill and going nowhere. So review this document periodically to ensure you're aligning with your company's business goals.

WHAT'S YOUR BUSINESS'S FLIGHT PLAN?

What's your business's flight plan? Where do you want to go, and how do you plan to get there? Partnerships are built on not just where your company *is* but where it is *going*. The core purpose of partnering is to grow the company, so your mindset needs to be broader than just your role. You need to understand the big-picture context of how partnering fits into the company's objectives. Essentially, you need to think like a CEO.

If your company is very organized and on top of things, a two-, five-, and ten-year plan might already be published and available. In many cases, though, you'll need to put on your detective hat. Review quarterly earnings reports, read the press about your company, and note important data points and ideas from all-hands meetings. Also identify and reach out to key stakeholders in your company who can help you better understand the internal corporate strategy and goals.

In your research, you'll be searching for the following information.

First, where the company wants to go. What's the BHAG (short for big, hairy, audacious goal, pronounced "bee hag")? The BHAG concept was introduced in the book *Built to Last* by Jim Collins and Jerry Porras. A BHAG is the vision for your company, even if it's so big that it seems unattainable. Not all teams reach their stated BHAGs, but some do. And one thing is certain: if you don't outline your BHAG, you will never reach it.

To reach that big, long-term goal, there will be smaller, short-term goals along the way. These are represented by key performance indicators (KPIs). KPIs are quantitative measurements, typically percentages, tied to a goal. What are your KPIs?

Within those KPIs, what is your company's North Star metric—the core metric that is the most important? Is it the number of users per year? Annual revenue? New regions your company's product or service launches in?

Now, what's the strategic business plan (SBP)? The SBP is the roadmap for how you will get to your target destination. It is a combination of three things:

▶ Value chain

▶ Go-to-market strategy

▶ Business model

First described by Michael Porter in his 1985 bestseller, *Competitive Advantage: Creating and Sustaining Superior Performance*, a *value chain* refers to the set of activities that a firm operating in a specific industry performs in order to deliver a valuable product (i.e., good or service) for the market area. The idea is to see a manufacturing (or service) organization as a system made up of subsystems, each with inputs, transformation processes, and outputs that involve the acquisition and consumption of resources (e.g., money, labor, materials, equipment, buildings, land, administration, management, etc.).

A *go-to-market strategy* is the plan of an organization, utilizing their inside and outside resources (e.g., business development managers, distributors, etc.), to deliver their unique value proposition to customers and achieve competitive advantage. The end goal of a go-to-market strategy is to enhance the overall customer experience, taking into account various aspects of the value proposition, such as the quality of the product and pricing.

Finally, a *business model* describes the rationale of how an organization creates, delivers, and captures value in economic, social, cultural, or other contexts.

This list is far from exhaustive, but there are four common business models:

▶ **Business-to-consumer (B2C), also known as direct-to-consumer (D2C):** In this model, individual customers directly engage with your product, service, and brand. You are accountable for delivering and supporting that end product for your customer.

▶ **Business-to-business (B2B):** This model involves a company providing a product or service to another business, rather than directly to individual consumers. Companies engage to address operational needs, impact expansion goals, or achieve value chain efficiencies.

▶ **Consumer-to-consumer (C2C):** This is where there is a platform for end customers to connect with other end customers that have a product or service to offer, like Etsy and Craigslist.

▶ **Business-to-business-to-consumer (B2B2C):** In this model, in order to reach your end customer, you partner with and engage a company that has better access to those target customers while developing a value proposition for that company as well as the end consumer. For example, car dealerships partner with Craigslist to promote vehicle listings, or companies post jobs on Craigslist for a fee.

These three components—value chain, go-to-market, and business model—are interlinked and will inform how you can most effectively partner. For example, to develop a sustainable and successful go-to-market strategy, you must understand the position your business has in the value chain that it operates in. Knowing your business model and go-to-market strategy helps you understand how you're currently reaching customers and can clue you in to ways you can either more effectively reach those customers or reach a different set of customers through partnerships.

With a good understanding of what makes your business tick, you'll be better able to identify the partnerships that will most help your company.

> **Know thyself.** Understand your company's KPIs and known gaps, as well as your strategic business plan.

WHERE'S THE TURBULENCE?

Now, in your flight plan, where do you expect things to be smooth flying, and where do you expect turbulence? Partnerships can be put in place to boost almost any internal effort that is not reaching its full potential due to feature gaps, resources, budget, or time. So let's first assess internal needs around what's important to your company. There are two exercises you can do to gain clarity here: a SWOT analysis and a core/context framework.

A SWOT analysis is a technique for assessing four aspects of your business:

▸ **Strengths:** What does your company excel at? What gives you a competitive advantage?

▸ **Weaknesses:** What is holding your company back from its maximum potential?

▸ **Opportunities:** What external factors could positively impact your company?

▸ **Threats:** What external factors could potentially harm your company?

A core/context framework helps you understand what is absolutely essential to your business that you cannot compromise (core) and what is not so essential (context). Geoffrey Moore articulated this core/context framework in his great book *Dealing with Darwin*, arguing that a company should manage these two different sorts of activity in fundamentally different ways. In addition to identifying what is core and context, further divide it into what is *mission critical*, meaning failure creates immediate and serious impact, and *non–mission critical*, which is everything else.

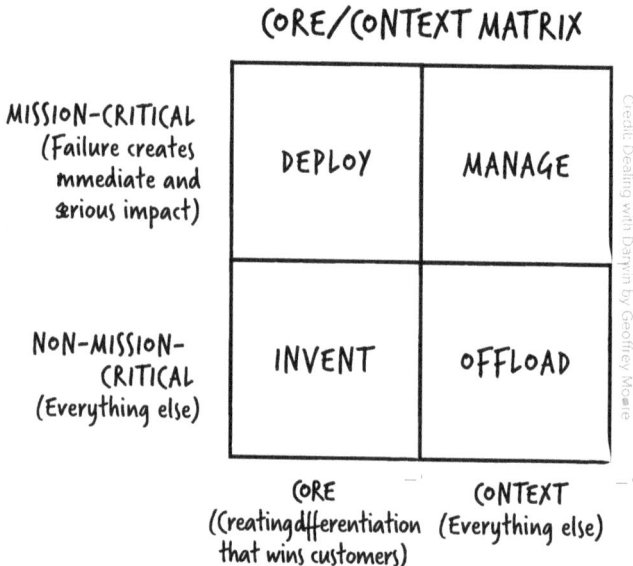

CORE/CONTEXT MATRIX

	CORE (Creating differentiation that wins customers)	CONTEXT (Everything else)
MISSION-CRITICAL (Failure creates immediate and serious impact)	DEPLOY	MANAGE
NON-MISSION-CRITICAL (Everything else)	INVENT	OFFLOAD

Credit: Dealing with Darwin by Geoffrey Moore

Later, as you start developing partnership concepts, you can come back to this framework to better understand the potential of the partnerships. The more mission critical a partnership is, the more impactful it will be for your business. That doesn't mean every partnership concept has to be mission critical. Sometimes partnerships are a great way to "offload" or outsource the non–mission critical things.

Take a mobile device company for example. Core to the company is a user-centric design and the quality of their device products. Meanwhile, the accessories for their device products—like phone cases and watch straps—fall more into context. The company might form a partnership with another company that provides the chips for their devices. That would be mission critical, falling into the "deploy" box, because if the chip fails, the entire device will not work. The mobile device company could also form a partnership with another company to create special branded straps for their watches (and in fact, mobile device companies *have* done such partnerships). That partnership would be non–mission critical and fall into the "offload" box. That doesn't mean it's not important, though. It could help drive the mobile device company's KPIs and get them to their BHAG.

So this approach is not meant to tell you to only do partnerships in a certain box of the framework. Rather, by identifying where the partnership falls, you know better how to manage it.

Both of these exercises come back to understanding your core business, which market area(s) you compete in, who your current and future competitors may be, and who your current and future target customers are. As you complete these exercises, keep these three big categories in mind, as these are the places where partnerships are typically most impactful:

▸ **Product:** How is your product competing in the market segment? Is there a clear leader? Are you close behind? Are you just starting out and need to play catch-up? Are there "parking lot" items for your product team, where they want to do something but just don't have enough time to get to it? Now a fun question: If you could give customers any feature or user experience (which you don't offer today in your product), what would it be, and what problems could it solve for them?

▸ **Marketing and branding:** What are your marketing goals for the quarter and year ahead? How do you feel you're tracking against those goals? What are the biggest challenges to reach those goals? How is your brand resonating with your target audience, and are there new audiences that you are going after? Now a fun question: If you could replace your brand/logo with another company's, what company would that be and why?

▸ **Distribution:** How do you distribute your product today? What are your distribution goals? What are the most effective channels for sales and ongoing customer engagement? Which regions are most effective? How are you better understanding what customers want within those channels? Why haven't you expanded distribution through other channels or into other regions? Which channels are underperforming and why? Now a fun question: If you could expand to any new customer segments or geographies that you're not operating in today, what would those be and why?

One word of caution: after you identify your company's gaps, you may be tempted to change your KPIs. Resist this urge. Feasibility should not get in the way of which KPIs are the right KPIs to grow your business. KPIs have many additional factors taken into account, including competition. So don't tweak and adjust your KPIs.

ARE YOU PARTNER-READY?

You've established your long- and short-term goals, outlined your internal plan, and identified the business gaps. Now it's time to answer a big question: Are you ready to explore partnership opportunities? Remember: in partnerships, timing is everything. It's about applying the right strategy at the right time.

Before partnering, you need to assess whether it's actually possible to deliver on partnerships. There are four major attributes to consider:

1. **Product readiness:** Has the product launched? If so, does it have the right features for expanding to new customers in new segments?

2. **Company capabilities:** Is there a team on board to execute partnerships, and if so, do they have the right skill sets?

3. **Feasibility:** Are teams fully allocated? For example, if your product and engineering teams are working at capacity and fully committed to existing projects for the next ten to twelve months, you're not equipped to create product demos and do product enhancements, and partnerships will be difficult.

4. **Product-market fit:** How many customers are engaged? Has the product become an essential part of customers' lives? Is your brand considered one of the top three to four solutions in the space?

> **First, "go at it alone."** Establish some product and customer success on your own prior to trying to attract prospects for partnering opportunities.

SO, CONSIDERING ALL THIS, ARE YOU PARTNER-READY?

It's okay if the answer is no. Just be proactive and focus on what you can do to become partner-ready. You might have the right product, but it's the wrong timing. Or maybe it's the right time but the wrong product. Or you could be partner-ready but only with smaller companies and not Fortune 500 companies. Whatever the situation, the important thing is to be realistic and focus proactively on what you and your company have control over. By focusing on what's in your control, your circle of influence (as Stephen Covey calls it) will expand, and you can become partner-ready.

WHO'S YOUR FLIGHT CREW?

If you want to build partnerships, you need a team to do it. The *partnership core team* will be the day-to-day team that works together on partnerships or a specific partnership initiative. Thoughtfully building this core team is crucial to ensure they are fully on board and committed to the partnership and related projects. This includes having the right representation from within your company and ensuring their leadership is aligned with their role and accountability as part of the partnership core team.

> 💡 **Create a partnership core team.** Partnerships don't create themselves. Build a team with clearly defined roles, including who will engage and secure partnerships and who will manage them.

In partnerships, there is a lot of ambiguity about who does what and when. Let's start with figuring out who the pilot and copilot are. The pilot is the person responsible for *creating* partnerships, and the copilot is the person responsible for *managing* partnerships.

Individuals that may be responsible for partnerships in a company, whether creating them or managing them, include:

▸ CEO (more common in smaller companies and start-ups that don't yet have a BD function)

▸ Strategic partnerships manager

▸ Account manager

▸ Business development manager

▸ Alliance manager

▸ Partnership engagement manager

▸ Sales manager

▸ Relationship manager

▸ And others

These job titles can be confusing because they're not well defined. They often mean different things at different companies and may have overlapping responsibilities. As a rough rule of thumb, if "strategic" or "business development" is in the job title, that person is likely responsible for establishing partnerships, whereas the other "managers" listed here are more likely to be responsible for managing the actual partnership. But when you're working with other companies, since so many titles are used interchangeably, it's good to ask questions to fully understand a person's role and scope.

To make things even more confusing, in many cases, no one individual is assigned to lead the partnership initiative. But it is crucial to have an internal leader appointed, even if unofficially. The partnership leader will not only act as the single source of truth but also ensure alignment around the common objectives and keep all teams and the initiative on target.

CO-ELEVATE METHOD FOCUS

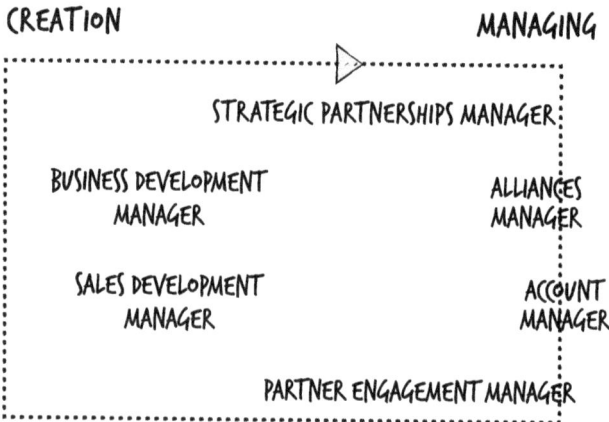

CREATION   MANAGING

STRATEGIC PARTNERSHIPS MANAGER

BUSINESS DEVELOPMENT   ALLIANCES
MANAGER   MANAGER

SALES DEVELOPMENT   ACCOUNT
MANAGER   MANAGER

PARTNER ENGAGEMENT MANAGER

So let's talk about the responsibilities of the pilot and copilot. Depending on the size of your company, you may have two separate people covering these roles or one person doing both jobs. These jobs require unique skill sets and have different goals: the pilot is a *hunter*, and the copilot is a *gatherer*. So if one person is covering both jobs, they need to switch between mindsets.

In hunting, your goals are focused on the results and impact of the deals you lead and close. Since partnerships may take one to two years or longer to launch in the form of a product or project, hunters need to gauge the *projected* impact based on a business case with outlined assumptions of the deal. Hunters are best at the big-picture, strategic thinking needed to create a great partnership idea and identify promising partners. They also need to be good at pitching their concepts and closing the deal for partnership agreements.

Gathering is about "farming" the partnership, ensuring a detailed execution plan is defined and delivered. Think of it like selecting the right crops from the farm and utilizing those resources for the success of the partnership. Gatherers are best at managing a partner-facing project from a defined scope to launch. They need to be good at building rapport and relationships and must know how to communicate effectively with internal teams that are technical and non-technical as well as external teams.

In addition to the pilot and copilot roles, you need the right mix of functions and expertise to fill out the partnership core team. The specific members will vary depending on your company and the types of partnerships you'll be pursuing, but here are some common roles:

▸ **A partner program manager:** This role is similar to a program manager but is a partner-facing role that is managing between external and internal teams. A partner program manager is essential to track all actions and schedules. They need to stay ahead about what's next and be assertive to ensure the teams (both the internal partnership core team and the partner company's corresponding team) are meeting deadlines and providing insight on the risks to reach crucial milestones.

▸ **A product or technical leader:** If there is a combined offering in the scope of the partnership, this person serves as your product domain or technical expert.

▸ **A go-to-market or marketing lead:** This person is focused on the end customer.

▸ **A finance lead and a legal lead:** Once you start engaging partner prospects, especially when contracts get involved, these individuals should be brought in to build a stronger foundation to the strategic partnership plan.

Note that once the partnership begins, each of these internal core team members must have counterparts in the partner's organization (though the exact job titles may vary) for seamless, effective management of the partnership. Without this core team in place, the partnership will have limited progress and success.

Remember that you can't make partnerships happen alone. Beyond the partnership core team, you need support from passive and active stakeholders across your organization. Partnerships start inside of your company before you can form them on the outside. Those internal partnerships are with your direct team; your peers and teams in the product, marketing, and operations departments; and with your C-suite, especially your CEO. Those stakeholders need to understand what your role is, what your plan is, and how you're going to help grow the company. Partnerships are not possible without the support of these cross-functional teams in every stage of the partnership, from the initial assessment and feasibility stages to the execution and launch to the long-term partnership management.

Assume that others do not know what you do and understand that their perception is likely based on their previous experiences with partnerships or business development teams and leaders, and who knows what those experiences were like? To build a good relationship with your internal partners, you will need to communicate a framework around how you think, assess, collaborate, and make decisions. This framework helps to build a mindset within your company and sets an expectation around what value your function may bring to the table. The Co-Elevate Method is a ready-made framework you can use.

WHAT'S YOUR PARTNERING STRATEGY?

We can now move on to the second layer of the cake: your partnering strategy. Defining a partnering strategy (the big-picture strategy behind partnering as a whole) is essential prior to outlining your strategic partnership plan (specific partnership initiatives). In the next chapter, we will look at how to develop specific partnership concepts, creating your Big Idea. A partnering strategy will help to guide and focus your brainstorming.

Your partnering strategy should be composed of three elements, built off the general strategy of your company's business:

▸ **Why you need to partner:** This relates back to the company BHAG or to the challenges and opportunities the company is facing.

▸ **How you will partner:** This is a high-level picture of how you will partner. We'll get more specific in the next chapter.

▸ **What impact you will make by partnering:** This is about how you will move the needle for the company and ideally connects to the core KPIs you identified.

For example, say you work for that e-scooter rental company. Your partnering strategy statement might be something like this: "To deliver an unmatched consumer experience and become the number one e-scooter provider in North America (*why*), we will partner with local and state municipalities, universities, and corporations to provide low-cost and highly available transportation options (*how*), increasing the number of daily rides with sustainability and safety as core operating principles (*what*)."

Be aware that your partnering strategy will change over time. Market conditions are shifting and changing at Mach speed. To continue to stay relevant and deliver value to your customers, you and your company must adapt and adjust your partnering strategy.

FROM STRATEGIC BUSINESS PLAN TO STRATEGIC PARTNERSHIP PLAN

One of the most critical parts of aviation is the *preflight check-list*. As defined in the *Human Factors* journal, "In aviation, a preflight checklist is a list of tasks that should be performed by pilots and aircrew prior to takeoff. Its purpose is to improve flight safety by ensuring that no important tasks are forgotten. Failure to correctly conduct a preflight check using a checklist is a major contributing factor to aircraft accidents."

Similarly, if you forget key tasks in a partnership, your partnership could be doomed even before takeoff. So at the end of each chapter, I'll provide a checklist to help you remember the key takeaways and decide whether you're ready to move to the next step. (Spoiler: These are the lightbulb notes found throughout the chapter.) Here's your first checklist:

▶ **Know thyself.** Understand your company's KPIs and known gaps, as well as your strategic business plan.

▶ **First, "go at it alone."** Establish some product and customer success on your own prior to trying to attract prospects for partnering opportunities.

▶ **Create a partnership core team.** Partnerships don't create themselves. Build a team with clearly defined roles, including who will engage and secure partnerships and who will manage them.

Now that you know what you want to achieve, you can start thinking about what partnerships could get you there. In the next chapter, we'll start brainstorming your Big Idea

CHAPTER 6

BRAINSTORMING THE BIG IDEA

A leading online recommerce marketplace I worked with wanted to broaden their distribution and grow revenue. They had achieved product-market fit, and there had been solid growth of gross merchandise volume (GMV) and number of transactions, which were their key success metrics. However, additional growth of the business was needed to capture the full potential of the addressable opportunity. It was the perfect time for a partnership.

We had determined the company was partner-ready, so the next big question was: What's the Big Idea, and who should we partner with on it?

I started with the North Star metric: gross merchandise volume (GMV). The more listings we had, the more transactions occurred, and the more revenue we made, so how could we get more listings? It was a two-sided marketplace with buyers and sellers, and the sellers were the ones who primarily help drive our GMV. We wanted to attract more sellers and get them to sell more items, so there was a lens shift to look at how to improve the experience not just for buyers but also for sellers. By catering to sellers that had more items to sell, the marketplace could unlock new growth opportunities.

I put myself into the sellers' shoes and did some research about how to get products onto commerce websites. I discovered that, in general, while many sellers pursue a top online sales channel, they don't want to rely on a single marketplace; they want to amplify their product listings across as many consumer touchpoints as possible. By using a variety of channels, sellers can reach more consumers and increase transactions. The challenge for sellers when working with several marketplaces is protecting their brand and having a consistent user experience.

Next, the CEO and I looked into the business ecosystem, researching how other marketplaces were growing their business. That led us to a category of companies called multi-channel listers (MCLs). MCLs allow sellers to streamline and automate their listings across multiple marketplaces at once while preserving their brand and customer experience. This was a promising opportunity for partnership. By partnering with an MCL, our marketplace could attract more sellers and thus further increase growth, distribution, and revenue. We had found our Big Idea.

We next had to figure out who to partner with. We ranked the major MCLs based on GMV and the number of sellers on their platform. The bigger and more scale the MCL had, the more reach and distribution amplification our company could achieve. We then ranked the top MCLs by which were the most hungry and motivated to bring our recommerce marketplace into the mix.

As a stand-alone marketplace, the question was how to work with MCLs who were already engaged with sellers as well as competitive marketplaces. MCLs provide optimized onboarding of a merchant's product catalog to a variety of marketplaces at one time versus working with multiple marketplaces independently. So I worked with MCLs to provide an onboarding kit to make it super easy for sellers to list their products on our B2C/C2C recommerce marketplace.

We succeeded in forming partnerships with several key MCLs, and this significantly increased the number of merchants and unique products offered on our marketplace, increasing both GMV and number of transactions, the key success metrics.

We all want to make a mark in this world and do our life's best work. It's not about checking the boxes and getting through the day; it's about building your masterpiece and finding your partner to develop an incredible solution, product, or service with that your company could not achieve on its own. Finding the right innovation partner is about first finding the right Big Idea and then finding someone who will fill in the gaps based on your company's strengths, weaknesses, opportunities, and threats.

BIG IDEA SPREADSHEET

To organize your brainstorming, I recommend creating a Big Idea spreadsheet. This will be your framework to assess your partnership concepts. You can design this spreadsheet the way you see fit, but as a guide, I recommend including the following columns:

▸ Category of Company

▸ Partnership Concept

▸ Partnership Objective (including the KPI(s) it will impact)

▸ Potential Impact

▸ Ideal Partner Profile

THE CREATIVE GEOMETRY OF PARTNERSHIPS

"Creative geometry" is a term my dad used to use. The idea is that we have lots of different dots (business inputs), and we can connect them in any number of ways, creating triangles, parallelograms, or any shape you want. In the initial brainstorming for your Big Idea, you will look at all the inputs and start synthesizing them, connecting the dots to create your own unique, transformational idea, whatever shape it may be.

The partnership team should work together on brainstorming. Keep the brainstorming sessions fluid and build the ideas as far and wide as you can. For now, all ideas are welcome. Don't be limited by what is feasible to build this year or what you currently have the budget for. These are ideas, and they don't cost your company anything at this point, but they could yield company-changing results down the road. Some of the ideas may be conceptual and abstract, while others are more tangible and real. That's okay. You will continue to develop the ideas throughout the Co-Elevate Method.

Dream big! Don't limit yourself. Brainstorm lots of partnership concepts, and imagine what those partnerships could look like in an ideal world.

There are two primary ways to brainstorm partnership concepts: in-out and out-in. This relates back to the idea of push and pull BD in chapter 3, "Building Partnerships as a Discipline."

For the in-out method, you start with a core company KPI, and you build out from there, thinking about partnerships that could help move the needle.

For the out-in method, you start with a partnership concept. This is okay, but remember: every partnership concept needs to tie back to a company KPI. The key to assessing what partnerships to work on and put time into is the potential impact to your business.

> 💡 **Connect every Big Idea back to your core KPIs.** To be successful, a partnership needs to have an impact on things that actually matter to your company. No matter how cool or interesting an idea is, if it doesn't move the needle on a core KPI, it's not a true Big Idea.

For example, I previously worked with a VR company that offers gaming experiences for groups through physical storefronts. We started with in-out brainstorming. The core KPI we wanted to improve was the number of customers coming to play at our locations. Though we had multiple locations across the country, the brand was still relatively unknown. So we knew we wanted to partner with someone who had a lot of brand recognition and an audience that would be interested in VR gaming. Simultaneously, we also did out-in brainstorming. One of our most successful games so far was one where we had licensed VR gaming rights from a popular science fiction book. Doing something similar for a partnership seemed promising. Combining our in-out and out-in brainstorming, we came up with our Big Idea: we could partner with a movie studio to adapt a popular TV series into an interactive VR game. This concept would allow us to tap into the show's existing fan base, driving awareness of our gaming experience and locations. Simultaneously, we would also help drive more viewing engagement for the TV series. This idea eventually led to a partnership with a major streaming service to adapt one of their biggest ongoing TV series. The game was a success, and the companies ended up developing another game together for a different series.

Ideally, you want a blended approach like this, finding the right balance between both methods. The in-out is about your company looking in the mirror, and the out-in is looking through a window first and seeing what the market and specific target partner prospects may need. If you look only from one direction, you'll overlook certain ideas, possibly missing out on the really great Big Idea.

Then, to add another layer to your brainstorming, you can think top-down or bottom-up. With top-down brainstorming, you're thinking at a high, strategic level. Essentially, what is the C-suite concerned with? With bottom-up, you're focused on tactics. What are practical ways partnerships could improve the day-to-day operations of your company?

PARTNERSHIP IDEA BRAINSTORMING FRAMEWORK

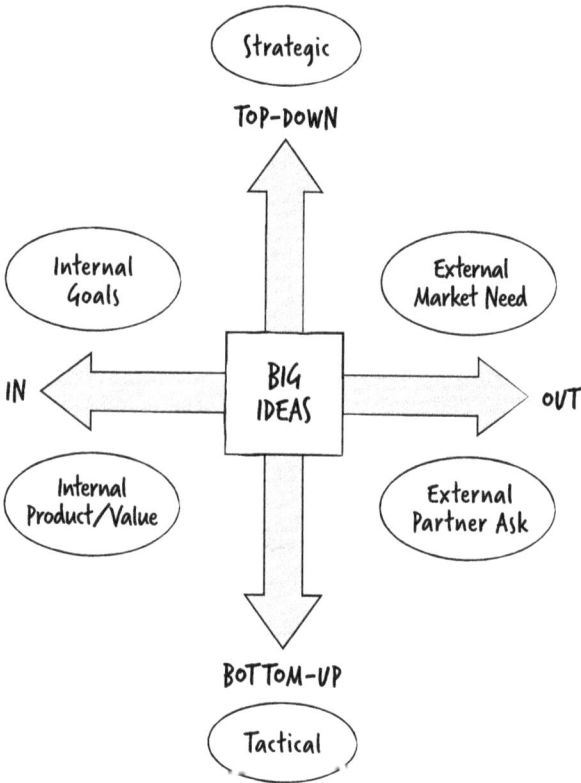

Strategic

TOP-DOWN

Internal Goals

External Market Need

IN ← BIG IDEAS → OUT

Internal Product/Value

External Partner Ask

BOTTOM-UP

Tactical

A final strategy is to look through a customer lens. Remember: you need partnership-market fit, meaning your Big Idea should address a need of a specific market. What does the customer need, and how could a partnership provide it? Typically, partnerships can provide one of the following benefits to end customers:

- A better user experience

- A better selection of products

- A better or new product offering

- Better and easier ways to engage with a product

- Better and faster availability of a product

Whichever brainstorming strategy you're using, don't focus on specific partner names yet. You need to focus on the "why" first and not the "who" in order to find the Big Idea that will impact the growth of your business. Later on, you will add specific partner targets to your spreadsheet. For now, just fill in the "Partnership Concept" and "Partnership Objective" columns.

Of course, in many cases you may not be in a linear process where you first develop a partnership strategy, then identify target categories of companies, and only then identify specific companies. You or your company may have already identified companies to engage with. That's okay—you don't have to start over, but apply the same level of diligence that happens in the linear process to wherever you are in your process. For example, perhaps a decision-maker in your company has already said, "Let's partner with Starbucks—they have tons of customers that want our product." The first question you should ask is, "Why would Starbucks want our product?" This will help you develop a win-win, better-together partnership concept.

If you're having trouble getting started brainstorming, refer back to the existing partnership models from chapter 4, "The Wide World of Partnerships." Can you tailor one of those models to create your own Big Idea?

WHAT GROWTH STAGE ARE YOU AT?

One of the key "dots," or inputs, for you to consider is where your company or an initiative is at in its growth journey. That can often give you an idea of what general types of partnerships you should pursue. Here are the four growth stages of a company or initiative:

▸ **Stage 1—Formation:** Your company (or initiative) is new and forming the initial team. The most viable product (MVP) is in development or recently launched.

▸ **Stage 2—Expansion:** The team's focus is on acquiring customers and developing audience reach. If you're a B2C company, initial search engine optimization (SEO) and search engine marketing (SEM) plans have been implemented. All growth is organic and through marketing and promotional efforts. If you're a B2B company, there are some initial sales underway with a certain market segment. You're starting to see consistent signs of positive market validation and product-market fit. You're also starting to explore geographic expansion to deliver the product or service outside of the current region you're operating in.

▸ **Stage 3—Maturity:** Financial results are consistent, and the business is operating at predictable levels. Organic growth strategies are starting to stabilize. The business is profitable and has been providing the product of choice in its category, meaning it has strong brand recognition and has become the default, obvious choice for many consumers.

▸ **Stage 4—Diversification:** Initial growth strategies have slowed, so to introduce new revenue streams and continue growing, your company (or initiative) is exploring new product lines and services surrounding the core product. You need to innovate to stay totally relevant. Your competition has outpaced you to capture opportunity as part of a new market transition. Your company (or initiative) has fallen behind, but there's still hope to shift focus where needed and to use your core assets. To reverse the decline, you need to cater to the changing needs of the customer today.

COMPANY/INITIATIVE STAGE

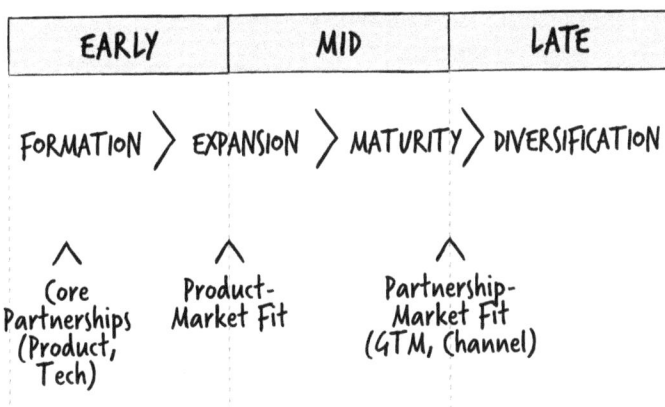

EARLY	MID	LATE

FORMATION > EXPANSION > MATURITY > DIVERSIFICATION

∧
Core
Partnerships
(Product,
Tech)

∧
Product-
Market Fit

∧
Partnership-
Market Fit
(GTM, Channel)

Now, here are some common partnership concepts for each stage:

▶ **Stage 1—Formation**

- Partnership for distribution for the initial launch segment
- Partnership for marketing, to tap into an existing customer base, for the initial launch segment

▶ **Stage 2—Expansion**

- Partnership for marketing, to reach new customer segments

- Partnership for geographic expansion
- Partnership for expanded distribution (channel partnership)
- Partnership for product enhancements

▶ **Stage 3—Maturity**

- Partnership for marketing, to reach new customer segments
- Partnership for geographic expansion
- Partnership for expanded distribution (channel partnership)
- Partnership for product enhancements

▶ **Stage 4—Diversification**

- Partnership for geographic expansion
- Partnership for expanded distribution (channel partnership)
- Partnership for product enhancements
- Partnership for innovation

WIDENING YOUR APERTURE: RESEARCH, RESEARCH, RESEARCH!

The only way to get ideas is by having lots of information, so you need to do research. This research will open up your "aperture" to what your market category and target customers really need. These insights will not only help you shape and re-fine your partnership concepts but also help you pitch your ideas later, as you'll be able to demonstrate a real understanding of the market dynamics. As much as possible, dig beyond broad market research to get a real "ear to the ground" understanding of what's working and not working in a given industry segment. This can define winning partnership ideas or alert you to where ideas could stop dead in their tracks—context matters!

> **Do your research.** The more information you have, the more and better ideas you'll come up with. Make sure to understand your business ecosystem and potential partner prospects.

There are three basic yet fundamental areas of a market segment to gather intel on:

1. **Market Scope and Trends**
   - How big is the market?
   - What is the current state of the market, and where has it been?
   - Where is the market going in terms of size?
   - What are insightful data points from adjacent markets that can help to explain the current and future growth potential?

2. **Audience Composition**
   - What is the demographic and psychographic makeup of the audience?
   - How has the makeup changed over a relevant span of time where meaningful shifts have occurred?
   - Is there a primary and secondary audience?
   - What can this data tell you about the future audience?

3. **Customer Activity Trends**
   - What is the audience doing?
   - How are they spending their time?

- How is the engagement with those activities trending?
- What are their new interests, and where are they being underserved?

There is no need to reinvent the wheel here. In many cases there will already be available research outlining the details of your ecosystem or the ecosystem that you want to engage in. For example, I once worked with a camping site marketplace, like an Airbnb for camping. I was not that up to speed on the camping market and ecosystem, so I started researching. After some preliminary internet searching around the market size and camping audience growth, I was reminded of KOA (Kampgrounds of America), which I had often seen mentioned in campsite reservations I'd made over the years. I looked them up and struck gold. KOA is the world's largest system of privately held campgrounds with almost five hundred locations across the US and Canada, and each year KOA publishes the *North American Camping Report*, which has a five-year outlook on the camping market. This report is public and free and had much of the information I was looking for.

Here's an example of the type of information I gathered, so you can understand the level of detail that is needed. The goal isn't to do the bare minimum of research just so you can push your idea. You want to become a real thought leader, able to connect the dots within the market. If you do that, people will naturally be interested in your ideas.

1. **Market Scope and Trends**

   - Since 2014, there has been an addition of an estimated seven million new camper households in the US, and the percentage of campers who camp three or more times annually has increased by 72 percent. RV ownership increased over borrowing or renting.

2. **Audience Composition**

- Both millennials and Gen Xers are more likely to identify themselves as lifelong campers when compared to past years.

- For the first time in the report's history, multicultural groups were the biggest and fastest growing segment of new campers.

- Half of all campers identified their "love of the outdoors" for sparking their interest in camping.

3. **Customer Activity Trends**

- While hiking/backpacking and fishing continue to be the most popular recreation activities among campers, more active recreation continues to grow in popularity.

- Interest in different types of experiences, including the establishment of "glamping" and "van life," has helped to further define camping today.

As you research, seek out real insights, something surprising that you can't really believe at first glance. The goal is essentially "tell me something I don't know." When scoping out a market and ecosystem, the value add from you is to synthesize the market into a collective group of insights that are relevant and meaningful to your business. Gather the relevant data into a summary of the market. Though it may be difficult, keep the information to a one-pager for now. Start by outlining an objective view of the market and then include a subjective view, *your* perspective of why the insight matters to your company. If this is a new market for your company to explore, share the one-pager with the relevant stakeholders in your company. Ask for feedback on what insights you should dig into further, and then build on areas that the collective team wants to learn more about.

After connecting the dots with the camping market research and analysis, a significant partnership opportunity was uncovered! Of course, campers need gear, and a major outdoor recreation brand and retailer was exploring ways to provide value-added services to their customers. It was a great match to give more people access to try camping for the first time and access special pricing for rentals. Eventually, the partnership was solidified and catapulted the camping site marketplace to its next stage of growth.

With this level of research completed, you can begin identifying partnership pathways within an ecosystem.

THE THREE "I"s: BUSINESS ECOSYSTEMS AND CATEGORIES OF PARTNERS

In the early brainstorming stages, focus on business *ecosystems*. A business ecosystem, as defined by Investopedia, is "the network of organizations—including suppliers, distributors, customers, competitors, government agencies, and so on—involved in the delivery of a specific product or service through both competition and cooperation." Understanding business ecosystems is key to determining the right partner. From business ecosystems, you can identify the categories of companies you want to partner with—the markets and industries that seem promising, like MCLs from the opening story. From there, you can further drill down to the companies you want to partner with, then the business units, then the teams, and finally the individuals and people to partner with.

Think about business ecosystems as a food chain, with many businesses interacting and dependent on one another. Map out all the steps that occur before the product is in the hands of the end consumer. What companies are involved—from manufacturers to suppliers to technology providers to distributors, marketers, and more? Think both vertically (the end-to-end creation of a product or service, like how a banana goes from growing on a tree to ending up on a supermarket shelf) and horizontally (the cooperation or acquisition of competitors at a certain level or stage within the vertical supply chain or more broadly across a range of industries).

From the food chain, you may discover more efficient and effective ways of partnering. For example, let's say you want to get your app on televisions. Your first thought might be to partner with consumer electronics companies. As you map out the food chain, though, you realize that most of those companies use original design manufacturers (ODMs). Instead of partnering with, say, thirty-plus different companies, you could partner with just seven ODMs and get the same reach. But wait. We can take this even further. What you really care about is the chipset in the television, and maybe there's only two chip companies in the ecosystem. With just two strategic partnerships, you could get your app onto televisions throughout the ecosystem. Now *that* is a Big Idea!

Keep in mind that your food chain today is different from how it will look in the future, so you may need to do this exercise again later. Also consider mapping out your competition's food chain, as this can give you good ideas for partnership concepts. Your competitors can serve as examples, but remember: the purpose of your strategy is not to emulate your competition but to differentiate from them.

As you build the food chains, the three "I"s—interrelation, interoperation, and interdependence—can help you uncover the ecosystem touchpoints and determine where to focus your and your company's energy. *Inter* is a prefix that means "between two groups," so each "I" represents a partnership dynamic.

▸ **Interrelation:** How do they connect?

▸ **Interoperation:** How do they work together?

▸ **Interdependence:** How do they depend on each other?

Once you have a handle on the food chains, you can begin drilling down into more detail.

To identify which categories of the ecosystem you want to target, start by determining your business heat map: Where are most of your customers engaging and why? What is so interesting to them? A feature? A use case? A brand attribute or characteristic? Partnerships can amplify your product and help you engage and reach more customers, but first you need to know what is already working so that you can identify the partners that make sense to engage with. Think about industries or types of companies in the ecosystem that do something you're not an expert in. Also think about your company's KPIs and your target audiences. Where are those audiences already engaged in large volumes? Where are they spending most of their time and wallet share? Where and how can they be engaged, so that you can bring your product to them in natural and authentic ways? In parallel, what are the biggest challenges for the ecosystem today, and how is it being disrupted? Knowing the threats and disruptions in the ecosystem can help to understand where your company can be of the most value to potential partners to offset those risks or to accelerate changes through technology or innovation.

As you identify categories of companies and even potential partners, add them to your Big Idea spreadsheet. Your win-win partnership concepts may be different per category but should not be too customized for each company target within a segment at first.

THE PARTNERSHIP SPARK

Sometimes you don't find the partnership concept; instead, it seems to find you.

One year, while I was advising an early-stage jewelry marketplace start-up, I attended a social media company's yearly conference. They featured some developers who had used their tools and showed how those efforts positively impacted the developers' businesses. They also demoed new tools being rolled out for creators (social influencers) and developers, showing examples in the fashion and beauty categories. That was when what I call the "partnership spark" occurred. I instantly thought of the start-up I was working with and thought, I want that to be us. I could envision us being a featured developer at this conference.

The partnership spark occurs when you consciously or unconsciously process research and insights that stimulate your imagination to create a new idea or an A-ha! moment. A spark alone is not enough, though. You need to fan it into a flame, turning it into a win-win partnership concept.

Think about what is most relevant and important to your prospect, and mold your concept around that. In this case, lots of companies want to be featured at the social media company's conference, to get exposure and gain access to better tools and more customers. We would need a way to stand out. Thinking like an executive of the social media company, I figured the best developer success story would be one utilizing not just a single tool but a whole suite of their developer services. So that's what we did, and it paid off. We were featured at the next big conference, which boosted our brand and audience, resulting in increased sales. It also attracted more creators and investors. And it all started with a tiny spark of an idea.

IDENTIFYING PARTNER PROSPECTS

Once you have an idea of the types of partnerships you're interested in, you can shift your focus to identifying specific partner prospects. Identifying partner prospects is not about quantity but quality. The goal is a short list of meaningful prospects.

Hunting for the right partners comes down to what your company really needs at this specific point in its growth. Is it more users? More promotions? New revenue? Better margins? Entry into a particular country? All of the above? When you think about what your company really needs, you'll start to see that only a few companies can fulfill those needs.

Start by building an ideal partner profile, a wish list of what you're looking for in a potential partner to make your partnership concept a success. Maybe you want a partner with great brand recognition or a large number of customers or cutting-edge technology or all of the above. Add it all to your spreadsheet. Right now you're focused on *wants*, not *needs*. So include everything, but don't expect to find a perfect partner who checks off every item on your list.

Then start creating a list of specific partners that meet all or some of your wish list items. Focus on partners that could complement your strengths or address your weaknesses. When you identify a potential partner, also look into who their competitors are, as those could also be target prospects. Add your target prospects to your spreadsheet, with one prospect per row. As you continue through the Co-Elevate Method, you'll make your partnership concepts more specific based on the prospect.

BIG IDEAS LEAD TO IMPACTFUL OUTCOMES

A partnership is only ever as good as the Big Idea at its core, so brainstorming partnership concepts is one of your most important jobs. Keep these tips in mind to come up with the best ideas:

- ▸ **Dream big!** Don't limit yourself. Brainstorm lots of partnership concepts, and imagine what those partnerships could look like in an ideal world.

- ▸ **Connect every Big Idea back to your core KPIs.** To be successful, a partnership needs to have an impact on things that actually matter to your company. No matter how cool or interesting an idea is, if it doesn't move the needle on a core KPI, it's not a true Big Idea.

- ▸ **Do your research.** The more information you have, the more and better ideas you'll come up with. Make sure to understand your business ecosystem and potential partner prospects.

At this point you have some good ideas and have even identified a few promising prospects. In the next chapter, we'll start pressure-testing and refining, zeroing in on which ideas and prospects to pursue.

CHAPTER 7

PRESSURE-TESTING YOUR BIG IDEAS

Once you have lots of ideas, your next job is to start pressure-testing, which has two purposes:

▸ To narrow your focus to one to three Big Ideas and a few top prospects

▸ To refine and expand your top Big Ideas

Pressure-testing will set you up for success in the next partnership stage, when you start pitching your ideas, and it can even give you new ideas or clue you into prospects that you hadn't considered before. In this chapter, we'll go through a number of different thought exercises and activities to pressure-test your Big Ideas. You don't need to complete these in order or necessarily do all of them. They are simply tools in your tool chest, for you to draw from as needed.

NARROWING YOUR FOCUS

Over time, you will hopefully pursue and form many partnerships, but you have to start somewhere. There are many factors to consider when choosing which idea and prospects to focus on first:

▶ Which partnerships have the greatest potential impact?

▶ Which partnerships move the needle on your most important KPIs?

▶ What level of work, time, and budget will each partnership require?

▶ How well does each prospect mesh with your culture and values?

▶ Which prospects offer the opportunity for multiple partnership initiatives and a long-term relationship?

There's not always a black-and-white answer, but there are many exercises that can help you gain more clarity. Before we dive in, create a new column in your Big Idea spreadsheet titled "Notes" in order to take—you guessed it—notes. You'll also be filling out the "Potential Impact" column. Okay, let's get into the first set of exercises.

CANDY, VITAMIN, PAINKILLER, OR VACCINE

To gauge the level of impact of the proposed partnership, ask yourself: Is the partnership concept a candy, a vitamin, a painkiller, or a vaccine?

A candy is sweet and tasty but has little nutritional value. In partnerships, a candy refers to short-term transactions that are nice but not very impactful. A vitamin, on the other hand, does have nutritional value. However, it is a supplement, a nice-to-have instead of a must-have. A vitamin partnership is typically not crucial but can increase or accelerate a desire or objective. A painkiller addresses a clear need. These partnerships solve a problem but may not have sustained strategic value. A vaccine likewise solves a problem but is designed to provide a long-term cure.

Focus on the painkillers and vaccines, not the candy or the vitamins. Essentially, ask yourself, "Can the company or initiative live without the partnership, or does it solve a real problem?"

This goes back to core/context (covered in chapter 5, "What's the Goal, and How Will You Get There?"). In some cases, partnerships can straddle both core and context, which is a double benefit and can make a partnership especially strategic.

WHO'S HUNGRY?

Not all prospects will be interested in partnering with you. You won't know the real potential of a partnership until you can gauge the willingness and capability of the prospect.

To make the best use of your time and resources, go after the hungry ones. They have a strong incentive to partner and will be more willing to make bets with you. The full up, satisfied ones can be hard to collaborate with, as they are already successful on their own and may not have the same drive to partner. Don't rule them out entirely, though. With a compelling idea, you could still form a partnership with transformational outcomes. Avoid the starving prospects, though. They may be on their last legs and may not have much to offer. Always ensure the prospect's core business is sound and healthy before pursuing a partnership.

Go after hungry prospects. For a partnership to succeed, both parties need to lean in, with the drive to partner and something compelling to offer.

PARTNERING DNA: MIRROR IMAGE EXERCISE

Understanding what makes your prospect tick is as important as knowing what makes your company tick. You want to get a sense of what I call their "partnering DNA," which is how they operate with partners. A company's partnering DNA is what determines why and how they make decisions with partners.

You and your partner don't need to be the exact same (and *shouldn't* be the exact same), but the partnership has better odds for success if you have shared values and compatible cultures. The most important thing is that if there are differences and potential points of friction, you are aware of them early so you can prepare for them.

A mirror image exercise will help you better understand your and your prospect's partnering DNA. Create two columns. On the left side, outline your company's partnering DNA, and on the opposite column, do the same thing for your prospect. Partnering DNA is composed of four big categories:

▶ **Strategy:** What are the prospect company's big goals, and what role does partnering play in achieving them?

- What are the top KPIs?

- How does partnering impact those KPIs?

- Is partnering a fundamental part of the business strategy or just window dressing?

▶ **Culture:** What is the prospect company mindset toward partnerships?

- How partner-friendly is the company?

- Has the company successfully partnered before?

- Do key stakeholders already believe in partnerships, or will they be skeptical?

- How does the company partner? Do they have a "better together" mindset?

▶ **Organization:** How is the prospect company set up to do partnerships?

- Does a BD team exist or only sales? Is there a partnerships team? If a BD or partnerships team exists, what level does that team report to?

- Does the leadership at the company have partnering or BD experience?

- How does the company make decisions—for example, is it based on data, executive mandate, relationship and trust building, or a combination of factors? Who needs to weigh in? If the partnership concept will require resources, who gives the approval?

▶ **Experience:** What partnerships has the prospect company already done, and what were the results?

- What products or services has the company launched with partners?

- What products or services is the company currently developing with partners?

- How did those partnerships turn out? Which were successes? Which were failures? Why?

You may uncover some eerie similarities or some daunting differences. Usually the assessment will fall somewhere in between.

Think about these attributes for your company as your persona, and your prospect has a persona too. Are you two friends with a lot in common and you're really going to get along, or will you (specifically *you*) need to be the interpreter between the two companies? I use the term *interpreter* since many companies even have a common language they speak and the terms they use can be different. You need to be that bridge, the translator who brings together two companies that may do business in a different way. This goes beyond a project or single initiative; it is about building a relationship.

Note: The partnering DNA is something you'll uncover and better understand as you start engaging with your prospect.

THE X FACTOR, SYNERGIES, AND MOONSHOTS

Remember: part of a Co-Elevate Partnership is that elusive X factor. You don't want a partnership that simply adds 1 + 1 to get 2. You want a partnership that creates something new that neither company can do alone, to give you 1 + 1 = 3 (or more).

Often you can uncover the X factor by searching for the synergies, or all the places where you and a prospect could work together for mutual benefit. You want to find multiple synergies across various parts of your business and your prospect's company versus only one or two areas. This is where you can become more "strategic" to a partner and a partner can become more "strategic" to you. Strategic in this context means having multiple touchpoints to a prospect's food chain, which can help to step change their business for the future. With more tie-ins, there is more potential "skin in the game" to have hard commitments from both sides to see real results.

Also think about moonshots: the big, ambitious ideas. It's good to have realistic initiatives that are feasible to execute, but ideally, a partnership should outlive an initial specific project. It should be a long-term relationship with many projects. Create a longer-term vision by identifying collaboration themes centered around evergreen areas where you and a prospect can work together and build value for each other over time. With this strategic focus, you can then brainstorm projects within a given theme, with each one building on the one that comes before. This allows you to paint the big picture with immediate, short-term ways to take action as well as longer-term projects for delivering fully on the vision. I have found that this approach enables higher-impact value creation for both companies over time.

Strive to be more than a transactional partner. Your company doesn't have the time, resources, or budget to waste on prospects that will not lead to big outcomes. Put that energy behind the opportunities that can become strategic and long term.

RANKING YOUR IDEAS AND PROSPECTS

Once you have identified a handful of the most promising ideas and prospects, you can rank them on objective and subjective criteria. This means doing more research. If it's a public company, look at the earnings announcements and dig into the latest annual report. If it's a private company, look through the website and research the founders and leadership team.

The objective criteria are the facts about the prospects, including data points such as:

▶ Number of users engaged (or subscribers)

▶ Potential addressable audience with your product or service

▶ Countries where they operate

▶ Number of physical locations (for brick-and-mortar companies)

▶ Any other relevant facts about the business

The objective criteria need to be quantitative so you can rank the level of potential impact to your business.

The subjective criteria are the qualitative attributes that help to assess the probability of executing a successful partnership with the prospect. Subjective criteria may include:

▶ Probability to engage the prospect's audience

▶ The prospect's expected interest level

▶ The prospect's execution capabilities (based on their teams' skill sets)

▸ The prospect's resource availability

▸ The prospect's marketing and promotional value for your company's brand

▸ Company culture compatibility

Which objective and subjective attributes are most important will vary depending on your business's needs at the particular moment in time.

After choosing your criteria, add them as new columns to the Big Idea spreadsheet. To keep it simple, subjective criteria can be gauged on levels of 1 to 3, with 1 = low, 2 = medium, 3 = high. These values aren't set in stone. As you engage further with your prospects, you will better understand their motivations and capabilities and can update the values to be more accurate.

When you have filled out your spreadsheet, use the sorting function to rank your prospects based on various criteria. Try to get a feel for the whole picture. For example, if a prospect scores 3s for all of the subjective criteria, that is a great sign, but how do they rank on the objective criteria that will move the needle for your business? After trying out a few different rankings, you'll get an idea of which criterion has the most weight. Usually, it is the prospect's scale and audience reach (number of users engaged or subscribers). Now leave the sorting on that column, add a new column named "Overall Opportunity Rank," and number the prospects from 1 to whatever number of prospects you have. This is a relative ranking among all the prospects in your spreadsheet. This is your priority list.

Remember: this is a living document that you should be updating over time, especially as you begin engaging with your prospects to understand their businesses and motivations. Also note that the opportunity rank doesn't necessarily mean you start with prospect #1 and work your way down. You may not be ready for prospect #1, and it may be better to start with #5 to test, learn, and optimize your approach and pitch. You want to be really ready and understand those blind spots before engaging with your top three targets.

REFINING AND EXPANDING YOUR BIG IDEAS

Now that you've narrowed your focus, it's time to further develop your ideas. When you present your Big Ideas to others in your company, they are going to have lots of questions. What are the benefits of this partnership? How is it going to affect our KPIs? Who are you going to reach out to? When? What resources will you need? The more prepared you are, the better you'll be able to answer these questions, and the greater your chances of success.

So let's dive deeper into your Big Ideas. Here are some strategies to further develop your concept into a winning Co-Elevate Partnership idea.

THE PARTNERSHIP MIND MAP

When you first start brainstorming partnership concepts, everything tends to get squished together into one vague, broad idea. A partnership mind map helps you structure the idea so that you can tell your story more effectively.

Place your Big Idea in the center of the map. Then create four branches:

1. **What** goal or KPI it will impact

2. **How** it will help achieve the goal or boost the KPI

3. **Who** to engage to achieve the goal or boost the KPI

4. **When** to engage the "who"

Off each of these four branches, you can include many ideas. The point is to get a full picture of the Big Idea. The "what" and the "who" should be mostly done already, so focus on "how" and "when."

The "how," at this stage, is a very rough business case for the idea. Take a "reverse engineering" approach. Start with the ideal end state, and then figure out the steps to get there. The "how" is key to your "why." By showing how the partnership will benefit your company, the prospect company, and customers, you can make a compelling case for why your company should invest in the idea.

For "when," think about the ideal timing for the partnership. Consider prerequisites needed before the partnership can begin—for example, maybe you have to complete something internally, like a product launch or make a key hire.

PARTNERSHIP VALUE DYNAMIC AND THE P-SWOT

The partnership value dynamic is based on the relevant capabilities each partner brings to the relationship, from product to brand to customer engagement. The goal is an *equal* value dynamic. This happens when the two partners bring something different to the table and are able to fulfill a need, or gap, of the other. This goes back to the win-win concept. Think about a magnet and how positive and negative poles attract each other, while the same poles repel each other. This is the basis for an equal value partnership.

There are perceived and real attributes of the value dynamic that should be made fully transparent in the early partnership discussions. The ultimate goal is for both parties to exert a mutual level of effort, but in the inception and early stages of a partnership, there is always an out-of-balance phase. One company is the *initiator* (the one giving the pitch and painting the picture of what could be possible in a partnership), and the other is the reciprocator (the one receiving the pitch). For the purposes of this book, I'm assuming you're the initiator. The goal of the initiator is to be fully aware of the partnership value dynamic prior to engaging with the *reciprocator*. That way, you can develop your pitch emphasizing your strengths, which are ideally the opposite of your prospect's strengths or something that offset their weaknesses. It's also key to outline the perceived strengths of the prospect and discuss them openly so that both parties are aware and in agreement on what the real versus perceived partnership value dynamic is. In addition, as the initiator, you should outline the threats that the prospect is facing, in order to frame the partnership as an opportunity. To do this positioning effectively, you must understand the state of the prospect's business, including competitive threats and consumer and market trends that can impact their core business as well as future growth potential.

Strengths, weaknesses, opportunities, threats—is this ringing any bells? That's right: it's time to do another SWOT exercise, specifically a P-SWOT, or partnership SWOT. This is a SWOT analysis of both your company and your prospect. Complete a P-SWOT for each of your top prospects (ideally three at most). This will help you understand what might drive your prospect to engage with you and your company, giving you more clarity about how to structure a potential win-win partnership concept.

There's one key difference between a P-SWOT and a standard SWOT. In a P-SWOT, each box is filled out from the lens of the other company and is focused on the partnership concept. So, for example, your company's strengths are not about your strengths in the marketplace and among competitors; they're the most desirable attributes that the other company could benefit from.

Gather as much current information as you can. Is there a recent announcement from one of their competitors? Is there a new hire inside their company leading a new team or initiative? What can you see from the outside to build a compelling win-win concept? Choose one top point per box.

Here's an example. An up-and-coming internet-based sports content company (we'll call it NetSports) is looking to engage with ESPN, one of the largest sports TV networks. Here's an initial P-SWOT:

COMPANY	NETSPORTS	ESPN
#1 STRENGTH	High millennial audience engagement	Live sports content rights
#1 WEAKNESS	Lack of content breadth and choice (specifically a lack of live sports content)	Limited audience reach (particularly among millennials)
#1 OPPORTUNITY	Increase viewing hours through a full-featured content catalog	Increase ROI of content licensing fees with broader audience engagement
#1 THREAT	Competition offering live sports via web, leading to customer switching	New audiences continue to engage on web-based services, impacting brand over time

Notice anything interesting? The #1 strength of each company counterbalances the #1 weakness of the other. Likewise, the #1 opportunity links to the #1 threat of the other.

This P-SWOT highlights a compelling partnership idea in which NetSports helps ESPN engage with a millennial audience, while ESPN helps NetSports expand their content catalog to include live sports.

A P-SWOT is a good way to understand the core reasons behind a prospect's motivations and cater to them.

GET TO KNOW THE PROSPECT'S PRODUCT

If you want to understand a prospect's business, you need to understand their product. The best way to do that is to become a customer. Use their product for yourself, if feasible. You can then incorporate your experience and feedback into your Big Idea.

At one point I was establishing a new relationship with a national retail club, so I joined their retail club, visited a store, spoke with their customer service reps on the floor, and purchased items. I told this story to the executives of the partner company the following day and shared my thoughts and takeaways from the experience. Becoming a customer will help you create strong and relevant partnership concepts. Plus you'll gain respect from your prospect, showing that you deeply care about understanding their business and audience.

Seek to understand the challenges of your prospect's business and how they may be underserving their customers. Based on your own experience as a customer, what new innovations can you offer that would make the customer experience better? Simultaneously, also work to understand what makes your prospect different and stand out from the competition. How can you enhance those strengths?

LOOK FOR A JOB AT YOUR PROSPECT'S COMPANY

Well, not literally! Looking at posted job listings is another input to better understand where your prospect may need help. Pay attention to leadership and organizational changes, as well as roles that may point to functional or strategic gaps. For example, maybe your prospect is hiring for a partner manager that is bilingual in certain languages and has experience in a specific industry or market area, or they're looking for an engineering leader with experience in specific coding languages or named technical platforms. The seniority levels and scope of these roles also provide insight into whether new teams are being built from the ground up or have plans for expansion to other geographic areas or industries. You'll need to connect the dots and synthesize this as another input into the state of your prospect's business.

PARTNERSHIP IDEA Ts

I've talked a lot about win-win partnership concepts, but actually, we can take it one step further: your partnership concept should be *win-win-win*. The number one priority is to create a winning idea for your end consumer, and the number two priority is that the idea is a win-win for you and your prospect. So that's three wins: end consumers, you, and your prospect. We can represent that with a diagram I call the partnership idea T:

Let's start with a needs T to outline what each party needs (for business growth or, in the case of the end consumer, a good experience).

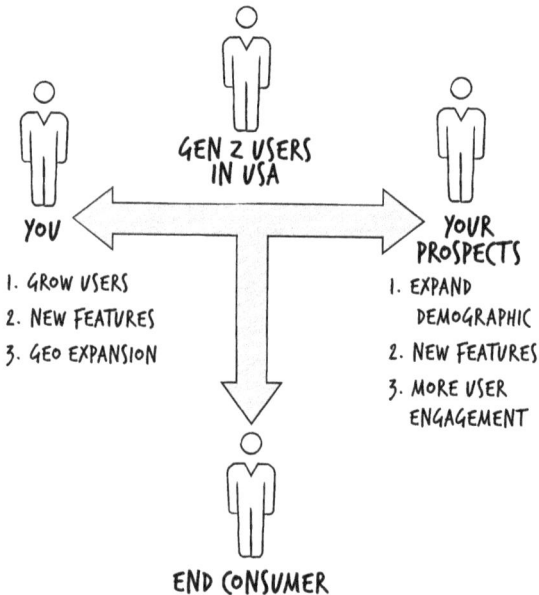

▶ **Step #1:** Write all of your needs on the left side of the T.

▶ **Step #2:** Write all of your prospect's needs on the right side of the T. Keep their KPIs in mind.

▶ **Step #3:** Write the end consumer demographic (age, region, etc.) at the top of the T and list the end consumers' needs at the bottom of the T.

▶ **Step #4:** Rank the needs for each party and place the number one need for each on the points of the T.

The T needs to be level. If there is a tilted T with no value or less value provided to one party, the T looks like this:

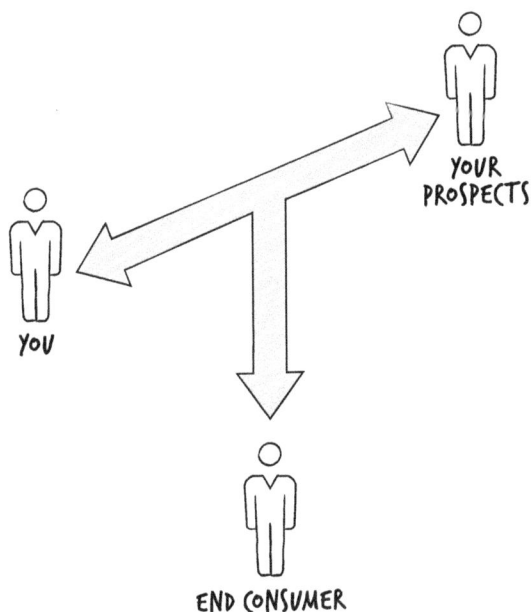

The most powerful partnership ideas need to address the needs of all three parties: you, your prospect, and the end consumer.

After completing the needs T, create a partnership T for your Big Idea with a specific prospect:

▶ **Step #1:** Write what you get out of the partnership on the left side of the T.

▶ **Step #2:** Write what your prospect gets out of the partnership on the right side of the T.

▶ **Step #3:** Write what the end consumer gets out of the partnership at the bottom of the T.

If you have a tilt to one side, try to find a way to bend the ends of the T to create more equality. Can you tweak the core idea, or add something to sweeten the pot for the party currently receiving less value?

Turn your win-win idea into a win-win-win idea. In a Co-Elevate Partnership, not only should both companies get value out of the partnership, but end consumers should benefit too.

LEAD PARTNERSHIP IDEAS

When pitching and discussing, both internally and externally, you should always—I mean *always*—present more than one idea but no more than three. Having more than one partnership idea allows the listener to react to the concepts by comparing and contrasting them versus just reacting to one idea. When you present only one idea, it's too easy to say no to it, and then your meeting is done. When you present more than one idea, instead of debating whether to explore a partnership, you engage in a mutual discussion about what the best elements of the concepts are. Avoid having too many options, though, because that can be overwhelming and lead to decision fatigue.

Share two to three lead partnership ideas. You should always present more than one idea when pitching, so based off of the Big Idea, come up with two to three ideas specific to the prospect.

The sweet spot is to have two to three lead partnership ideas. You want to bring the most impactful partnership ideas to your prospect, so first assess the ideas on their impact. Think company-changing concepts, not incremental ideas or enhancements.

Each of these concepts should include multiple related ideas. The more quality ideas for collaboration between two companies, the better. Some of the ideas will be more candy or vitamins, but the foundation should be all about the painkillers and vaccines. Think of concepts that can help grow your prospect's business in several ways, and frame the concept around how you're going to win in the category together. Remember: you're looking for a partner that your company can work and evolve with over time. It's not about the upcoming quarter or year ahead; it's about the next two to five years or even the decade ahead. This type of long-term positioning sets you apart from being a vendor or supplier and instead a true strategic partner.

After assessing impact, assess *effort*. Companies like to see what level of impact and growth they can achieve with the least amount of effort in the shortest period of time and then replicate that effort to further scale the business. In your prospect meeting, plan to show two versions of the partnership ideas: one outlining the impact and one outlining the impact plus what would be required (at a high level) from both parties to deliver on the partnership ideas. The impact must be meaningful enough to justify the level-of-effort investment, which includes budget, resources, and time. A partnership idea could have massive impact, but if it takes too long to implement or costs too much to develop or the needed resources (e.g., team members) are already allocated on other projects, there's a good chance it will be rejected. An optimal partnership idea includes sizable and measurable impact that can be recognized in the shortest period of time without additional resources or budget. Only if all partnership ideas could be like that! Well, sometimes they are. This is where your preparation and planning come into play. Work through multiple scenarios internally and then outline those partnership ideas in their simplest form to review with your prospect.

As an example, when I was leading partnerships for a startup company, we developed three concepts to discuss with the prospect:

1. Co-brand a product solution based on an existing product where we (my company) do all the development and sell the product through the prospect's sales channels

2. Create a new product solution that addresses the most untapped consumer need

3. Create a joint innovation lab where both companies can incubate ideas

By presenting multiple ideas, we created choice through options to build on. In this particular instance, we actually ended up pursuing all three of these ideas with the partner, so this method also has the benefit of expanding the partnership to a longer-term relationship.

Sometimes you might not have entirely different concepts to present. That's okay. Create variations by modifying one or two ingredients of the concept, like time or initial scope.

Keep in mind that at this stage, these ideas are just that: ideas. They can be morphed and changed and built on, so be flexible internally and with your prospect. The point right now is to better understand the needs and priorities of the prospect.

IDEA AND IMPACT HEADLINES

Whenever you're introducing a new idea, you want to make it as simple and easy to understand as possible. So put on your marketing hat to come up with some memorable headlines.

First, for each lead partnership idea, come up with an *idea headline*: a short, crisp headline explaining the "what" of the idea. The headline is the better-together story summed up in a single line. It should be aspirational and focus on the benefit to the shared end customer. For example, let's take the Apple Watch Nike partnership. You could say, "An Apple Watch with Nike design and integration," but that's not very compelling, is it? Instead, you could say, "A 24/7 digital personal trainer on your wrist." Now that's an idea people will want to get behind.

Next, create an *impact headline* that encapsulates the "why": the big value that could be achieved. To do this, start sizing the business impact of the concepts. At this point it's not about completing a full business case and analysis of the deal. It's a high-level, initial forecast of the impact to your company's core metrics. Here are some example impact headlines:

▸ Increase the number of transactions by 20 percent in the first year, resulting in doubling gross merchandise volume by year two

▸ Through a new partner product, introduce a new $10-per-user revenue stream in North America by year two and for all worldwide customers over time

▸ Access to ten million subscribers with the potential to engage 50 percent of that user base

Hang on to these headlines because you can and should use them when you start presenting your ideas internally and engaging with prospects.

PRESSURE MAKES DIAMONDS

By pressure-testing and refining your ideas, you can turn them into diamonds, and diamonds are much more compelling than lumps of coal. Here are some key takeaways before moving to the next stage:

▸ **Go after hungry prospects.** For a partnership to succeed, both parties need to lean in, with the drive to partner and something compelling to offer.

▶ **Turn your win-win idea into a win-win-win idea.** In a Co-Elevate Partnership, not only should both companies get value out of the partnership, but end consumers should benefit too.

▶ **Share two to three lead partnership ideas.** You should always present more than one idea when pitching, so based off of the Big Idea, come up with two to three ideas specific to the prospect.

Now that you've refined your ideas and identified a few target prospects, you can start pitching and discussing your ideas. Before approaching your prospects, though, you need to pitch and discuss internally to gain alignment.

ALIGN: TAKING FLIGHT

CHAPTER 8

ALIGNING INTERNALLY ON THE BIG IDEAS

Previously, I led partnerships for an internet video company. One of my favorite parts about this position was that every quarter I would meet one-on-one with the CEO to sync up. These meetings were short but incredibly impactful to my job. I would come prepared with partnership ideas and strategic questions to get the CEO's guidance, and I would walk away with clarity on the paths forward.

One of those CEO meetings in particular stands out to me. I was working with our device partners to get a button for our streaming service added to their remote controls. One of those device partners had recently partnered with a hotel chain to provide all the televisions for their guest rooms. Our device partner proposed bringing us into this partnership, providing a special guest experience for our streaming service on these televisions. For example, when a guest checked in, if they had an existing account with us, they would automatically be signed into the TV in their room. If they didn't have an account, they would be signed up for a free trial. Sounds like a win-win-win, right?

Well, when I brought the idea up with the CEO, his feedback was to not distract from our priority goal and to stay on the path and approach we had agreed on. If we stayed on that path, our streaming service would end up on all of our device partner's TVs anyway.

Fast-forward to today and the streaming service is available on TVs at not just the hotel chain from this story but many others as well. Staying focused at that critical juncture helped us to achieve far more than we would have with that single partnership idea.

The key lesson of this story is how crucial it is to gain perspectives and reach alignment with your internal partners. Your internal partners are the cross-functional business unit leaders that either have to approve the partnership or will be involved in the execution of the partnership—the CEO and executive team, engineering, product, marketing, sales, customer service, and whichever other teams are required to make the partnership successful. Your internal partners are the *most* important partners to achieve success of your partnership strategy and plan because without them, external partnerships are not possible. Your internal partners also bring valuable expertise and wisdom that can ensure you're pursuing the right partnerships at the right time. In this example, the fact that there wasn't internal alignment was like a giant flashing neon sign saying, "Don't do this." If I had tried to push ahead with this partnership without the CEO's insight and alignment, it almost certainly would have failed. Instead, by focusing my efforts on the partnership concepts that *did* have internal alignment, we were able to achieve great results.

Alignment, both internally and externally, takes work. You should expect tension both with internal stakeholders and partner prospects. Relationship tension goes with the territory when proposing change, especially new innovations that may rethink and shift the status quo. Internal tension is common when the proposed Big Idea could impact an internal product roadmap and operating plan, an organizational or team structure, or a service or technology built in-house. Externally, I find that tension is particularly common when you're attempting to elevate a current "customer" to be a "partner." These tensions are natural and can be healthy, as long as you don't ignore them. Addressing the tension is a constructive way to build trust.

This all starts internally. You need to influence and sell your internal partners on your vision for why partnerships—and specifically your Big Ideas—are critical to the growth of the company. In this chapter, we'll go through strategies and tips to achieve that internal alignment. As an added bonus, these tools will also serve you well as you start to share your Big Ideas with partner prospects.

SUSPENSION OF DISBELIEF

When introducing new ideas that can have transformational impact, the amount of change required—from an existing mindset to organization to strategy—can be significant. While you may clearly see the potential path to achieving the idea, not everyone else will. They may not have the same access to research, experience in a given industry, or spectrum of imagination due to current priorities on their plate. Others may be more skeptical and not believe in the idea due to existing norms or assumed roadblocks. That means part of your job is to create a "suspension of disbelief," which is a concept borrowed from literature, film, and the like. The idea is for the audience to let go of logic and critical thinking and allow themselves to believe what may seem unreal or not possible in reality. For example, with a movie, the viewer ignores the fact that they are watching a camera filming an actor on a movie set.

We can apply this same concept to partnerships to shift mindsets and alter what seems possible. Steve Jobs was a master of this. The Apple team that worked with him on the first Macintosh idea and development even coined a special term for it: the reality distortion field (RDF). The RDF was Jobs's ability to convince himself and those around him to believe in almost anything by distorting what previously seemed impossible. As a partnership leader, try to create your own RDF, bridging the gap between your Big Idea and the reality.

The key to suspension of disbelief is to remove anything that is so glaringly impossible that the audience simply cannot suspend disbelief. With the movie example, if you have a boom mic hanging right in the center of the shot, the viewer is going to have a hard time forgetting that they're watching actors on a set. In partnerships, there is a point at which the constraints become too much for people to envision the partnership becoming a reality. In order for your audience to suspend disbelief, you need to address the potential limitations. Work to understand the biggest concerns that the skeptics may have. What is preventing them from suspending disbelief and supporting the idea? Is it a missing skill set needed for the partnership idea? The amount of time required? Lack of executive alignment? Identify the roadblocks and then provide pathways to resolve them, to make the idea seem more realistic and possible for your audience. As you do this, you must weigh the level of change and the cost of that change with the potential impact of the partnership idea to justify the required effort. In other words, is the juice worth the squeeze?

A good strategy is to recruit internal champions that have influence internally as well as domain expertise in the area of the partnership idea. They can help you hone the partnership idea and navigate the internal organization to achieve alignment.

> 💡 **Ensure you have a champion (with an influential position in your company).** You need to get people on board with the partnership. Trying to influence and get buy-in from the bottom-up is a hard uphill battle. It's more effective to bring in others that have already built credibility with the decision-makers for the ideas you're exploring.

Let's face it: we don't all have the same charisma and bravado as Steve Jobs. Over time, though, you can hone your own persuasion style and techniques that work for you.

THE PARTNERSHIP MOCK PRESS ANNOUNCEMENT

A good way to help your audience suspend disbelief, as well as to get clear on your partnership concept and envision what it would look like in action, is to write a mock press announcement. This isn't a term sheet; it's a partnership vision and concept. It's a short summary document you can share first with your internal stakeholders and then later with your prospect to get their reactions. Engage and work with your PR team on this exercise. Bring them along for this journey early so they will understand the partnership vision and become part of your core team.

To write the mock press announcement, ask yourself, "If the partnership goes through, what would the partnership announcement look like? What does it say? Who is quoted in it?" Thinking about how the partnership would be presented publicly gives you a clearer picture of the partnership vision. For example, the headline of the mock press announcement indicates the impact of the partnership. The main body of the mock press announcement outlines the purpose of the partnership, from the values each company brings to the relationship to the product or service the companies will be collaborating on. Who is quoted provides context about the "why" and the scale of the partnership. If the partnership will impact the companies at a corporate strategy level or even impact the industry as a whole, possibly the CEOs are quoted. If the partnership is within a business unit or for a product line, the related executives may be quoted.

Now, looking at the mock press announcement, do you still believe in your concept? Is it impactful enough for your business? Is there enough value in it for your prospect to engage and be interested?

Assuming your answers are yes, you can share the mock press announcement with your "friendlies" internally (the people who already support the idea of partnership). You don't need to share the nitty-gritty details of your ideas and concept yet. Focus on the big picture that is provided in the mock press announcement, and use their feedback to revisit your assumptions and ensure you are on the right track. Specifically, ask your friendlies what they think about your company's and your prospect's motivations to engage in the partnership.

ELEVATING AND ALIGNING WITH EXISTING ENGAGEMENTS

In some cases, there may already be a relationship or existing partnership within your company with the prospect you want to pursue. This can be a tricky situation, as you will need to navigate those existing relationships. Anytime there is an existing engagement or relationship, it is critical to first align internally with the teams currently engaged with the prospect and to understand the state of that relationship.

Each situation will be unique, but generally, partnerships will fall into one of these four categories, which come with different engagement approaches:

▸ **Net new partnership:** There is no existing business relationship or partnership between the two companies.

Thus, this is a net new engagement between the parties, and there will be a cold outreach and steps to establish the relationship and partnership over time.

▸ **Existing team-to-team engagement:** There is already an existing sales, supplier, or partnership relationship with the partner organization. In this case, be sure to connect and align with your internal contacts first and understand the state of the engagement. For example, who is doing what (between your company and the partner)? What is the sentiment of the relationship — is it positive or not? What level of the organization is engaged on both sides of the partnership in terms of teams and company hierarchy? Pay attention to other learnings about the partner's organization, culture, and strategy. Make sure to not cross communication wires with the existing engagement with your new partnership ideas. Keep the new ideas separate and potentially with an alternative contact at the partner company. Be sure to stay internally aligned on the process and progress.

▸ **Existing C-level sales engagement:** There is already an existing engagement at the C-level, but it is not strategic and more on the sales or supplier side. Dig in and do your homework on the existing agreements in place. In this situation, your goal is often to shift the narrative of the overall engagement and relationship to include a strategic mission that combines the existing engagement and your new partnering ideas. You can use a broader multi-partnership framework where more than one partnership workstream may be occurring in parallel.

▸ **Existing C-level strategic partnership:** There is already a strategic partnership at the C-level. This partnership can provide valuable learnings for how new partnership ideas may be explored or evolve. Also, your internal contacts that are already engaging with the partner company will likely have valuable insights for how the partner operates, from decision-making to execution. This scenario provides the opportunity to introduce your new partnership ideas into the existing strategic partnership. If there is not an established process to do this, work with your current partnership lead for the company to create a process and align on a path to introduce the new ideas at the leadership levels.

In short, always consider the existing engagements. Look for ways to amplify the existing relationships, and use your internal contacts who could help to influence decisions or provide guidance on how best to explore the new partnership ideas. Particularly if there is an identified leader from your company who interfaces with the external company, you will need to collaborate internally to develop a game plan together. If the existing relationship is having challenges with progress, an alternative approach may be just what is needed to increase visibility or impact. Consider reaching out to different partner teams at the external company or shifting the narrative of the relationship. Sometimes, even if the existing engagements are going smoothly, there may be opportunities to do more together with other teams or in different areas of the partner organization. There may also be an opportunity to elevate new partnership ideas at the C-level, but be cautious not to be perceived as if you're escalating to executives or bypassing the existing partner teams. Take the time to preserve the existing relationships that your company's team members have developed and build those relationships further.

COMMUNICATE YOUR VISION

To gain internal buy-in, you need to communicate your vision. I've experienced that some partnering functions lack strategic context and primarily focus on execution with specific partners, which can result in missing opportunities, not seeing blind spots, or being seen as just "winging it." By communicating your vision, you can show your internal partners not just "what" you're doing and proposing but "why."

Yearly or quarterly planning meetings are a great time to lay out your partnership plan. Before you present the plan to a wide audience, schedule one-on-one pre-wire meetings with the most important stakeholders—i.e., the cross-functional business unit leaders who will be involved in the partnership initiatives. They will be more receptive if they feel in-the-know prior to the larger meeting. Scheduling one-on-ones helps you build your relationship with them and also gives them a chance to provide you feedback.

Then, to make things easier, here's an outline of a slide deck or document for you to follow in the larger planning meeting. This is only a directional template for you to tell your story, so customize it for your company culture, audience, and whatever presentation style and material format you're comfortable with.

1. The Impact of Partnerships

If you haven't done any partnerships yet, you can skip this section but there's a good chance you have partnerships already in place in your company. Do a quick look back on how you did last year or last quarter before going into what your plans are for the future. How did partnerships impact the company, especially core KPIs?

2. What You Learned

Again, if you haven't done any partnerships previously, you can skip this. Otherwise, outline what went well and what could be improved. How have you taken the past experience into account in building this new plan?

3. Company Mission and Partnering Mission

Include the company mission (even if it may be totally understood). Then include your partnerships mission.

Your partnering mission should enable the success of the company mission. This is your time to explain that you're developing partnering activities to help grow the overall company. This shows alignment of company and partnering missions. As an example, a partnering mission might be, "We will grow our customer base in the US by 15–20 percent through partnerships over the next two to three years. We will continue global expansion and introduce our products in Germany through a strategic partnership with a regional company."

4. Overall Company Strategy

Reiterate the overall strategy for the company, using the known vocabulary and sticking to the strategy visual that your audience knows. Again, while your audience knows this already, it is good to reiterate to show that you know it as well and that it is the basis for your partnering strategy.

5. Main Partnership Growth Initiatives

Overlay the opportunities for growth through partnerships on top of the overall strategy visual, indicating where those opportunities inject and accelerate the velocity of your overall growth.

> **Nail the "why" in plain simple English.** Write down the "why" for partnering in a super simple way. It should be something that others in the organization can relate to and that can be communicated without the message changing like through a game of telephone. Say it out loud, tweak it, and make it short and easy to remember.

6. Potential Impact on Core KPIs

Next include the potential impact to the core KPIs. Show the percentage of total impact from partnerships compared to the overall growth story of your company or team.

Don't commit to specific numbers or metrics here. Instead, include a range and explain the assumptions you're making and known risks to achieving those goals.

7. Partnership Core Team

List who is on the partnership core team, and outline their skills and expertise. Then indicate what percentage of their time is put toward the main partnership growth initiatives. For example, do they spend 100 percent of their time on partnerships or perhaps only 10 percent? If it's relevant, also include how much of their time is focused on a specific partner.

8. Specific Prospects and Partners

Categorized by the main partnership initiatives, include a dashboard of specific prospects and partners.

9. Partnership Scenarios

Now lay out your strategic partnership plan, which requires building a more robust business case for the Big Ideas. Do some financial modeling, both for the costs of the partnership and the potential impact. Think about who will need to be involved to make the partnership happen, how long it will take, and what monetary resources will be required. For example, maybe it will take a team of ten engineers six months to build the integration with the partner, along with a $5 million marketing budget. Then map out the predicted impact on the KPI, revenue, customer experience, and so on. Think about this through not only your company's lens but also your prospect's lens.

Present two scenarios:

1. **Your plan of record (POR) track:** what you can do *with current approved resources and budget*

2. **Your go-BIG track:** what you could do *if you had more resources and budget*

For scenario #1, you're applying internal constraints, which provide a less risky, more predictable path. This is your realistic plan, tied into the overall goals of the company.

Scenario #2 is the "what-if" scenario that removes barriers of feasibility around resources, budget, and other constraints. Scenario #2 is normally what your CEO wants to see. It is your chance to paint a picture of how partnerships could make the biggest impact possible to the company. This is your partnership BHAG (big, hairy, audacious goal). Lay out a question like, "How do we increase growth (e.g., users, revenue, etc.) through partnerships by 10x?" This will capture the imagination and engage your audience in a creative exercise.

For scenario #2 you're outlining the internal support that would be needed in order to have greater outcomes. The partnership business case and impact must exceed the resource and budget investment over time. Build out the scenario #2 business case to show the *crawl, walk,* and *run phases* of the partnership ROI plan, including the scope of each stage (e.g., audience size, geography, etc.):

- ▸ **Phase 1—Crawl:** Outline bite-size partnership ideas that provide options to quickly and easily start seeing results.

- ▸ **Phase 2—Walk:** Outline how you will start scaling, optimizing, and expanding the breadth and depth of the partnership impact.

- ▸ **Phase 3—Run:** Outline the big, ideal end state as the overall North Star for the partnership.

Crawl, walk, run! Start small with one partner with one product in one region. Paint a big picture of how you're both going to change the world together, and then group the plan into stages that are part of an overall journey.

For example, perhaps the crawl phase is formation and initial launch, the walk phase is optimization, and the run phase is when the partnership is operating on a global scale. Along with these phases, include the incremental resources and budget required to enable this scenario #2 plan. Phase 1 of a go-BIG partnership scenario will not justify additional investment, so paint the longer-term picture. Also paint a broad picture, thinking not just about the future ROI of the specific partnership but also the possibility of that partnership opening up other partnerships, after serving as the first initiative to test, learn, and optimize with.

10. Your Asks

End with your specific *asks* for your audience. What do you need from them to achieve success in your function? Be sure to explain how you will engage with them to ensure they are aware of your progress. Remember that you will not be successful without your internal teams and support from your manager and CEO.

> **Gain internal alignment.** Communicate the "why" and use your internal champions to get folks on board with the new partnership initiative.

GET THE FLYWHEEL MOVING

In *Good to Great*, Jim Collins explains that driving a new strategy is like getting a huge flywheel into motion. Initially, there is no movement. Many people think the strategy is absurd, and it is almost impossible to imagine the flywheel at speed. With great exertion of will, though, you can get the flywheel started. At first the movement seems small and trivial, but it provides the credibility needed to move to more ambitious results. As more and more results accumulate, more and more people throw their weight behind the wheel, and the momentum of the flywheel builds and builds.

It will take effort and time to get your partnership flywheel moving, but stick with it, and you'll gain inertia and speed that allow you to coordinate and execute partnerships more smoothly. Your internal relationships are the bedrock for your success, so complete this checklist before moving to external prospects:

▶ **Ensure you have a champion (with an influential position in your company).** You need to get people on board with the partnership. Trying to influence and get buy-in from the bottom-up is a hard uphill battle. It's more effective to bring in others that have already built credibility with the decision-makers for the ideas you're exploring.

▶ **Nail the "why" in plain simple English.** Write down the "why" for partnering in a super simple way. It should be something that others in the organization can relate to and that can be communicated without the message changing like through a game of telephone. Say it out loud, tweak it, and make it short and easy to remember.

▶ **Crawl, walk, run!** Start small with one partner with one product in one region. Paint a big picture of how you're both going to change the world together, and then group the plan into stages that are part of an overall journey.

▶ **Gain internal alignment.** Communicate the "why" and use your internal champions to get folks on board with the new partnership initiative.

Once you gain internal alignment and are given the go-ahead to proceed, you can start engaging your target prospects.

CHAPTER 9

THE PARTNERSHIP PITCH

I still remember the exact day I learned one of my most important lessons about partnerships. It was a rainy day in South Korea. I was a part of the team leading partnerships for an internet media company, and we were working with an electronics company on a new smart TV platform initiative. In order to close the deal for our partnership and launch together, we had to lay out realistic details of the schedule—specifically, we had to figure out if our platform would be ready in time for the release of the next year's TVs. So, we went to our prospect's headquarters for a collaborative planning session to outline what a joint schedule could look like.

Our prospect shared a detailed month-by-month schedule with us, including where they thought their biggest risks were in the schedule. With TV hardware schedules, there is no moving of the launch dates. You must hit the date for the retailers to carry the next model year TVs. On our side, we were dealing with software, which has a bit more schedule flex but still required milestones be in place for integration and testing. We were still building our software platform, and we didn't have our engineering team in the room with us, so it was hard to provide specific dates. More importantly, we couldn't commit to adjusting our dates based on our prospect's needs and schedule.

Frustrations started to rise, until our primary contact stopped the meeting and said loudly, "Where is your principle of reciprocity?" He had a valid point. From his perspective, we were not being equally as transparent as their team was.

We took a break to cool off, and I talked with him one-on-one. He explained that he wanted us to be more open about our schedule, even if we didn't know all the details yet, and I assured him that we would get him the answers he needed and gave him a specific date we would have them by. Before we went back into the meeting, I talked with my team privately and told them that we needed to open up more. I emphasized that while it's not okay to provide inaccurate information, it's also not okay to simply be quiet and not answer the questions at all. Instead, you can simply say you don't know and you'll get back to them.

This simple mindset shift to reciprocity made a difference. By being more transparent—even when that simply meant admitting we didn't know but would find out—we were ultimately able to close the deal.

A partnership requires a healthy business relationship. You need to be on good terms to work well together. But what does "good terms" actually mean, and how can you create it? It's what our TV partner contact said: the principle of reciprocity.

Reciprocity is about give and take. It is like an exchange of "currency" between two parties. If one party extends currency and the other party does not reciprocate, then there is a debt. The more debt that builds, the more the relationship suffers. The currency of a relationship can take many forms. It is anything that is important to your partner and to you. It could be information, time, resources, or something else. You extend currency whenever you put your partner's interests before yours. An equal exchange of currency is how both parties know that you both care. You must find out what your main contact's preferred currency is through understanding what motivates them, and then you want to fill up their relationship "bank account."

Successful engagement of a prospect is about building a relationship, which all comes down to trust and respect. In this chapter I will be taking you through a step-by-step process of engaging a prospect. In each step, keep the principle of reciprocity in mind.

DECIDING WHO TO CONTACT

The first big question to ask is: Who are you going to contact? If you don't select the right audience for the right ideas, your Big Ideas won't get off the ground. Be aware and cautious of engaging the right prospect and partner teams for the proposed partnership. Do your homework to understand how decisions are made at your prospect company. What would need to happen in order for your Big Idea to be agreed to and executed?

Remember: transformational ideas are disruptive. Tension is to be expected, but you want to avoid outright opposition. For example, let's say your company has a technical solution to propose to a prospect. If you reach out to a team that is developing its own competing solution, they won't have a strong incentive to engage with you. You'll often need to do research to find the right contact, particularly since job titles can be misleading in the partnerships space.

If you have an existing relationship with the company, then you may already have a good contact. Otherwise, there are a few different approaches you can take, each with pros and cons:

▶ **CEO (or other C-level leader):** Reach out to the CEO or a relevant C-level leader.

  • *Pros:* The buck stops with the CEO. They are the key decision-maker. (Depending on your ideas, the partner's board of directors may need to review and approve the initiative, but the CEO may still be your best place to start.) A CEO will have the broadest strategic lens, and if you can build a relationship at the top, the partnership is more likely to become a priority. In some cases, another C-level leader could be a good choice as well—e.g., the executive responsible for a business unit relevant to the partnership or for a function that spans across the company, like the chief operating officer (COO), chief business officer (CBO), or chief revenue officer (CRO).

  • *Cons:* Executives are busy. For this approach to work, you will need a very compelling partnership concept and introductory message. The idea must be something they would care about, like a concept that could help alleviate pressure from a competitor or get their company out ahead in the market segment. The concept should be strategic and long term, not a transaction. Think like a CEO here: Why would it make sense for the CEO or another executive to take time out of their busy day to discuss this partnership with you?

▶ **CEO to handoff:** Start with the CEO again, but instead of requesting a meeting with the CEO, ask them to hand you off to the best internal contact to discuss the concept.

  • *Pros:* Since CEOs are busy, this approach puts the idea on the CEO's radar while requiring only a small amount of their time and effort. If your outreach message is compelling, the CEO can simply forward it to a team member. Since the message will be coming from their CEO, the team member will most likely respond. The idea might impact that person's team and business unit more directly, so they may have more interest. They may also need to provide their CEO an updated status of the outreach and engagement.

- *Cons:* The partnership idea may have limited relevance to the new contact, or they may not have enough influence or decision-making approval to green-light it. Beware of this situation, as your outreach could hit a wall and not progress forward. You may want to have the new contact help schedule a CEO-to-CEO meeting instead of trying to fully explore the next steps with the new contact.

▶ **Working team:** Start with a member of a working team related to the partnership idea.

- *Pros:* Reaching out to and developing a relationship with a member of a working team gives you the opportunity to learn about the organization's culture, like how decisions are made internally and with partners, who is influential at the company, and who makes decisions for the types of ideas you've developed. These insights are invaluable and can help you adjust and tailor your pitch to have the most relevant impact.

- *Cons:* It may be hard to make progress within a working team, and it may be hard to break through into higher levels of the organization, in order to have a discussion with an executive decision-maker. You also may end up getting paired with this original contact long term, and that established relationship may be hard to change until there is a reorganization in the prospect company's team.

▸ **Domain expert:** Start with someone who knows a lot about the areas related to your partnering idea.

- *Pros:* Engaging with a domain expert can provide valuable insights on your partnership ideas, including how the company's internal systems operate, how its products are built, and so on. This valuable information can help you hone your ideas and potentially make them more relevant to the partnering organization. Domain experts are often influential in their organizations. If you get them involved in the idea, so that they feel some ownership of it, they can become champions for the idea internally.

- *Cons:* You may become too focused on the product and technical areas of the idea versus the strategic impact and longer-term business value. You also need to do your homework and ensure you are reaching out to the right expert team members; otherwise, you may not be spending your time building the most valuable relationships to help you and your prospect.

So, which approach is right for you? It depends on the partnership concept. The idea drives the outreach plan. You want to get in touch with whoever the decision-maker will be for the partnership concept. Depending on the level of impact the concept has, that will most likely be a business unit leader or the CEO. Ensure you're starting at a VP level or above. The higher you go in the organization, the broader perspective you will hear, and you can then be connected to the right individuals within the company to talk to. You should also consider your own position. Ideally, you and your day-to-day contact at the prospect company will be at similar levels, in order to increase the odds of a response. Upleveling is important, though, to ensure that the partnership opportunity has visibility in the company and that the appropriate effort and resources are allocated to it.

Consider the previous example between NetSports and ESPN. Since the partnership concept is about live sports, a good contact would be the C-level executive responsible for content instead of someone in, for example, legal or marketing. You could take the "CEO to handoff" approach to get in touch with the content executive, while also asking the CEO's guidance for how best to explore the idea, in case they have someone even better in mind.

If your prospect has an existing partner program and the partnership concept is within the bounds of the program, then you should contact the head of that program. But don't let your partnership idea be put in a box! Paint a picture around how you can be the number one success story for the partner program and emphasize that you want to be innovation partners and collaborate in a way to help your prospect evolve their program.

As you're trying to find the right contact, you may come across hybrid sales and BD roles, but beware: they may be more sales than BD at first glance. If there is no BD counterpart at your prospect, go higher in the organization to a strategy or relevant business unit leader or the CEO.

Also, regardless of who your initial contact is, the CEO is always the top decision-maker, so you should always try to put the partnership concept on their radar, even if most of your engagement will be with someone else.

Once you've identified your contact, it's time for more research. Get to know who your contact is and what motivates them. Look into their background, where they have worked, where they went to school, press release quotes and mentions, public interviews they've done, and so on. LinkedIn is a good resource to understand their roles and job history as well as find common connections. Who do they report to, and who reports to them? How is their name mentioned in articles versus interviews—for example, if their name is Saoirse, how do they pronounce their name? Is there a short form name they prefer? If you can't find this information online, ask them directly or wait until they introduce themselves and then write it down phonetically so you remember it. Nuances like how you address your contact are important. All the "little" things really add up, and some of the things you may believe are little are actually the big things that will make or break the relationship in the early stages.

CRAFTING YOUR OUTREACH MESSAGE

In an ideal world, you will already have a relationship established with your contact, perhaps through networking events or past working relationships. The importance of having first a relationship and then a trusted relationship must not be underestimated. Presenting a partnership idea to a "cold" contact is much more difficult than with existing, trusted contacts. If you can, first take the opportunity to develop rapport and a relationship prior to jumping right into your partnership ideas. Take the time to get to know your contact and understand them and then their business.

Building on existing relationships is the ideal route, but life is not always ideal. In many cases, the first contact will be online, through email. If their email address isn't clearly listed on their LinkedIn or the company website, there are third-party services that provide research on organizations, including job titles and email addresses.

Make it easy for your prospect to imagine a future together. Help your prospect visualize what new value you can bring customers together by writing a personalized message.

Starting a relationship through an email is a challenge, so you want to be thoughtful about your outreach message. You can customize the following three-part message structure for your specific situation and desired outcome.

1. **Intro:** Explain who you are, what you do, and what the company you work for does.

2. **Your Big Idea in context:** Include a short statement about your idea and how it benefits the prospect. Make it impactful and highlight how your company is best situated to enable that impact.

3. **Why now (optional) and an open-ended question:** If there's a reason you're reaching out now, include it—for example, maybe there's a company milestone in the near future or an industry event that you and your contact will both be attending. Then close with an open-ended question asking for a simple and quick response about next steps.

First, let's look at an example of what *not* to do:

> *Hi [CEO], could you please connect me with your decision-maker that is responsible for making purchases of new products and services?*

There is no intro, no why, and no intriguing idea. There is also no human connection made. With a message like this, you will likely not get a response. So let's try again:

> *Hi [CEO], we have some new ideas to help you sell more of your products to customers. How can we set up a time to discuss these new ideas?*

Better, but needs more work! What are the ideas? Where's the hook, for the CEO to want to learn more? What is the benefit for the prospect and their customers? At this stage, you want to evoke intrigue, and give a sense of the potential impact. Time to rewrite and rewrite again.

Now let's look at some good examples. Here's one reaching out to ESPN's head of content, John:

John, I hope this email finds you well. I lead strategic partnerships for NetSports, a sports-based content destination with more than [#] views per month and a strong millennial audience (include # if meaningful). My CEO has an idea to explore with ESPN around providing what you offer to your customers to NetSports' millennial audience. We would love to hear your feedback on the concept. Could you let me know how best to approach a conversation with ESPN on this topic?

Your help is much appreciated, and thank you for taking the time.

If you recall, ESPN's top weakness was lack of audience reach among millennials, so this message is likely to catch their attention. Note that the message doesn't call out ESPN's weaknesses but instead emphasizes NetSports' strengths. Your contact will already know their company's weaknesses and connect the dots on their own.

Here's another example of a message I actually sent (edited for privacy purposes):

Mark, I hope this email finds you well. We're now working with your company on a longer-term partnership to get you connected with the start-ups we're engaged with. In the short-term I have a really interesting opportunity sparked by a partnership idea to share with your company. I wanted to give you an early sneak peek to this since I think it could be a standout for bridging online and in-store experiences. The demo should be ready in early February, and I would love to have my CEO talk you through our offering and demo. What would be the best way to schedule that time?

A couple of things worked well in this message. First, I referenced our companies' existing partnership to build trust and credibility.

Then I used the idea of a "sneak peek" and short-term impact to create intrigue and urgency. It worked, and I got a positive response.

Here's another message I actually sent (again, edited for privacy purposes):

> *Melissa, it was great to meet and talk at the conference! Congrats on all of the amazing progress and announcements. We're cooking up some new things here and would love to share some ideas with you around how my company and yours could make a dent in the developer universe together. Would you be up for 10– 15 minutes in the next few weeks? If you're up for it, let me know how best to schedule.*

This is a good example of how to follow up from an in-person meeting. The message was conversational and started with a personal connection, reminding her who I was. Then, instead of diving right into the pitch, I took the time to first congratulate her to further build rapport and demonstrate the Co-Elevate mentality, in which you truly care about the success of your partner, on both the company level and the individual level. Then, knowing she's a busy person, I made a clear but small ask. She responded and connected me with her head of business development.

Here are some additional tips to keep in mind when crafting your initial outreach message:

▸ **First impressions matter.**

- If you can, get an introduction. Do any of your company's senior leaders have existing relationships at the company? Or do you have a common investor, board member, or shared contact that could provide an introduction?

- Take your time to write and revise this message. Sleep on it before you send it, and consider having internal colleagues provide feedback.

- The subject line is your very first impression. It can make the difference between your target opening up your email or sending it straight to the trash. As a starting point, try something like "Hi [contact's first name], [your name] from [your company]." If your company isn't well known, you could instead mention a common investor or contact.

- Be intentional about when you send the email. My recommendation is to schedule it to send at 7–8 a.m., so they see it when they start their day, before their inbox is flooded with emails.

▶ **Keep the message simple and short.**

- You don't need to share too much information and detail. Keep it to the golden nuggets that could help their business progress and differentiate.

- Use simple words and sentence structure. Stay away from acronyms and technical terms.

- Note that your recipient may receive the email on their phone. Keeping it short makes it easier to read through on a smaller screen.

▶ **Make the message conversational and personal.**

- Tailor the message for the recipient. Don't just copy and paste the same message to multiple contacts.

- Tone is everything with email, especially when it's your first interaction. Try to be conversational but not overly casual, which could seem disrespectful. Imagine you bumped into your recipient at a conference and you're having an impromptu conversation. (But remember to keep it brief and to the point.)

- Include their first name as well as yours for the introduction.

▶ **Be intriguing while keeping it professional, and include data points.**

- Be humble yet ensure you communicate your company's success and progress with relevant data points, to increase your chances of getting a positive response.

- Try reverse-engineering your message based on what your prospect needs. Is there any public news about challenges the company is facing? The P-SWOT is a great starting point to help develop the right data points and counterbalance points.

- Position your ideas to help address your prospect's challenges, but don't directly call out their issues, which can be off-putting. Focus on your value-adding ideas.

- You need to make it worth the recipient's time to respond. Try to make the recipient feel they could be letting go of an interesting opportunity if they don't respond.

▶ **Make it easy to respond.**

- Include a simple question that engages your recipient to respond.

- Don't ask the recipient to commit to anything or respond directly about the partnership concept. Instead, ask for their advice on how to explore the idea further.

▶ **Remember that this is only the first email.**

- Again, don't cram too much into the first message. You'll have a chance to share more information.

- The goal of this initial email is simply to get a response, not to get a meeting scheduled. Don't worry—that will come soon.

- Think about this as a conversation. You send a message, they respond (possibly including another team member), you respond with the idea of meeting up, they include their executive assistant to set up an initial call, and so on.

▶ **Follow up.**

- If and when your recipient responds, include a high-level yet time-sensitive message that further paints a picture of the opportunity to work together and create a sense of urgency to get the ball rolling on further follow-up.

- No response might mean the prospect isn't interested, but it could also mean that they missed the first email, or it slipped their mind, or they're not the right contact. So, if you don't get a response after one week, it's worth following up. You might also consider trying someone else in the organization. Be sure to revise the message before doing so, as they may have been forwarded the original message, and you don't want this to seem like an impersonal, cookie-cutter message.

Crafting this initial message takes time, but it's time well spent because it leads you to an introduction call.

> 💡 **Don't put all your eggs in one basket.** Get various irons in the fire and let them all heat up. Put optionality in effect, which is "the quality of being available to be chosen but not obligatory."

THE ULTIMATE FIRST CALL

The initial introduction call is crucial to set the tone of the relationship. This is your chance to cement a good first impression as well as ask those introductory questions that you can't ask later in the process. It's also an opportunity to build your credibility and trust with the contact. Try to make the introduction call one-on-one, so you can make a direct human connection.

You still don't want to share too much detail at this point. Keep it strategic and tied to the big KPIs. The goal is to further frame the partnership concept and show how the relationship could be complementary. The information you receive is just as important as the information you give, so you can better understand your prospect's partnering DNA.

The following are the key areas and questions to cover. Note: This is a dialogue, not an interview. Make it reciprocal. As your contact talks through their answers, share your answers too. The more you share and the more transparent you are, the more the other party will feel comfortable to open up and engage with you. (Remember: Reciprocity.)

▶ **Getting to know each other**

- How long have you been at [their company]?

- What's your background? Where did you join from?

- What was your biggest reason for joining [their company]?

- What is your role at [their company]? Who do you report to?

- What are your goals for your role? What does success look like for *you* (not just the company)? (As part of a win-win concept, you not only want both companies to win but both partnership teams as well. Your goal should be to make your contact successful, so find out what is most important to them for their job.)

- How would you describe the state of your function (e.g., forming, building, growing, scaling)?

▸ **Framing the conversation and the objective for the call**

- Explain your reason for reaching out and expand on the initial concept shared via email. Don't get into the details at this point. Focus on the objective and outcomes of the concept and what the implemented solution could provide to the prospect.

▸ **Understanding each other's businesses at a high level**

- What are the objectives and strategic priorities for your business?
  - Talk about the relevant short-term (6–12 months) and longer-term (12–24 months) initiatives under way.
  - Also talk about the biggest relevant challenges for each company.
  - Stay humble. You may be talking about your company's traction and success where the prospect may not have traction and success (yet).
  - Explain that you are seeking out the right partnership with the right company. This lets the prospect know that they could potentially miss an active time window for the opportunity.
- How do you measure success, and what are the KPIs for your business?

▸ **Understanding each other's partnering DNA**

- Can you tell me a bit about how your company views partnerships and business development?
- Has your company done a partnership you are really proud of? Can you walk me through what that looked like?
  - This will help you understand what is most important to your prospect when it comes to partnerships. You want to better understand what worked and emulate those positive and effective parts.

- Get details, from how the successful partnership was structured from a day-to-day operating perspective to how goals and objectives were measured.

- Have you had a partnership effort that didn't work out? Why do you think it fell short?

  - Knowing the prospect's partnering history is extremely helpful when determining how best to partner with them now. This gives you a view into the blind spots that you could accidentally stumble into.

  - You'll also uncover the political current and dynamic in the organization around partnerships, including open wounds or already formed opinions about what doesn't work with partners. Knowing where their battle scars are and comparing yours with theirs can be a healthy process to help you most effectively design the partnership framework.

- Who are the key influencers and who is the final decision-maker for partnerships?

- What do those stakeholders see as the most important content in order for them to say yes?

Really get to know your prospect and how their leadership team operates. Get to know the culture through your partnership detective work. Understand what their CEO is most concerned about and who their competitors are. Find out about recent partnerships they have engaged in and how those engagements are evolving.

As you wrap up the introduction call, try to make a personal connection to build rapport and trust. Talk about any upcoming travel you have or a big company milestone you're celebrating soon. Now is the time to tee up the next meeting, which should also be one-on-one if possible. Ask them where they are located, and depending on the distance and the importance and potential impact of the opportunity, you could suggest going to them and meeting face-to-face if they're up for it.

At this point you're not asking for anything in return. You're providing information and giving context. Be patient to hear back from the prospect. Don't be pushy—give them space and provide a comfort zone to have an enjoyable and meaningful dialogue with you.

Build trust with prospects by taking turns peeling back one layer of the onion at a time. Relationships are built on reciprocity. The more transparent you are, the more transparent your prospect will be (most of the time). But only share what you need to share that will benefit the partnership, and don't share everything all at once. Build the relationship over time, with several calls and meetings.

ALIGNING ON THE CORE ELEMENTS OF THE PARTNERSHIP

In subsequent meetings, you can start nailing down more details. Remember: a Co-Elevate Partnership is like creating a new virtual company with two teams from two separate companies. This new entity needs planning, structure, and leadership to know what success looks like and the path to get there.

First, design a *Partnership Objectives and Principles (POP)* list with your prospect counterpart. List the objectives of the partnership and prioritize them around what is most important to them and you. Then list the partnership principles—how and why your two companies should partner. The principles will help each of you understand what you're looking for in a partner as well as your culture and brand value match. Beyond the product, audience, brand, or whatever business value you and your prospect bring to the partnership, the way your companies get things done and how decisions are made are critical to building a partnership for the long term.

Be upfront, honest, and transparent with this step. Remember the principle of reciprocity. The more transparent you are, the more transparent your prospect may be. Openly discuss both your cultures and then identify shared values as well as unique values that will remain independent but should be recognized. As I've said before, you don't need to have the exact same cultures. But making a partnership work is all about the "chemistry." If that chemistry doesn't naturally exist from the start, then you need to recognize it and figure out a way to create a winning combination of company cultures. It is also totally okay to walk away (gracefully) at this stage of the engagement. It is much harder to "break up" once you've committed and put in more valuable time and resources, including setting internal expectations in your respective companies.

Based off the objectives and principles, create a shared partnership mission statement. You can use the vision, mission, strategy, and objectives (VMSO) model. The vision should be aspirational and somewhat unattainable. The mission is what you're going to do. The strategy is how you're going to do it. The objectives are the KPIs or goals you will achieve. Try to keep it to three to four big benefits or outcomes.

Also create a *Partnership Core Team (PCT)* proposal with your counterpart indicating who will be working on the project and partnership, with specific names and titles.

Once your POP is complete, decide together how best to share it within your companies and with the individuals that will be part of the partnership initiative. After you are aligned on the core elements of the partnership plan—the Big Ideas, the POP, the PCT, the rough timeline, and the next steps—you and your contact will be ready to host the joint partnership pitch and discussion.

NAILING THE PARTNERSHIP DISCUSSION MEETING

This partnership discussion meeting is the big, critical opportunity for you to sell your vision for the partnership so that the two companies can begin officially and formally exploring the partnership ideas. You often get only one shot to present your ideas, so make this meeting count!

If possible, plan this meeting with your prospect contact. You can also ask them to co-present the opening slides to help frame the discussion together. You know when you're at a car dealership checking out a new car model and you feel like you're being harassed by a salesman? I call that pitch pressure, and no one likes it. By co-presenting, you relieve the pitch pressure, gain credibility, and position the meeting more as a discussion versus a one-sided *Shark Tank*–like pitch.

Start with your shared partnership VMSO. From there, create your meeting objectives: what you want to accomplish in the meeting. This first meeting is about creating a relationship and engaging the audience in the combined story. The big objectives are to (1) discover what is important to the prospect and whether the partnership ideas can help them achieve *their* desired goals, not yours, and (2) set up another meeting. It's not realistic to walk into the first meeting with a prospect for one hour and walk out with agreement to sign the term sheet, though it *can* happen. Realistically, strive to walk out of the first meeting with heads nodding the right way to tee up the next meeting. Let's dig into some tools and strategies to make that happen.

TELLING YOUR STORY

I have sat through so many presentations and meetings that were not engaging and not actionable. Even if the ideas were good, the presentation killed all the potential excitement. To prevent that happening to you, at a high level, think about the narrative for the meeting in the form of a story arc. Stories are fun and compelling, and it's a great way to get your audience invested and excited about your ideas.

Every story is different, but there are three main "acts" of a story in the business context of a meeting

▸ **Act One**—Framing: Set the scene and introduce your audience to the characters, the setting, and the seeds of conflict. Explain who you are as a company and why you exist (the characters). Then talk about the state of the industry—the competitive landscape and the consumer disruptions currently occurring (the setting). Finally, explain the Big Problem you and your company are seeking to resolve (the seeds of conflict). This should be a problem that your audience cares about. No one likes being sold to, but they pay attention if you tell them how you're going to solve their problems.

▸ **Act Two**—The Meat: Lay out what you do and why it matters. Show how your company has been addressing the Big Problem and gaining traction, with your solution growing and changing in response to consumer needs. Then, for your meeting audience to understand your story and how they fit into it, you need to make them part of it. Emphasize how the Big Problem will only become more of an issue for the world, so you need a partner to work with to solve it for customers and help people live better lives.

▸ **Act Three**—The Ideas: Show how the characters, including your audience, resolve the Big Problem. Really paint a picture of what's possible. Then, as the story ends, tee up the actionable next steps together. Think about how you can foreshadow the "sequel" to this first story and meeting.

With an understanding of the story arc, you can start creating a presentation storyboard, which is a simple way to lay out the flow of the presentation and meeting before developing the specific content. Think of it like an outline for your slide deck or an agenda for the meeting. Slides are not always the best tool to use live in the meeting depending on the audience, room size, tone, atmosphere, and so on, but they are a good way to sequence your thoughts. They give you a palette to work with and develop your ideas around to ensure you cover your main points when in the room.

To make your presentation storyboard, you can use whatever software you normally use to make a slide deck, but personally, I've found the most effective way is to get about fifteen pages of blank white paper. With physical paper sheets, you can zoom out and see the overall flow, and you can easily move things around as you develop the content. On one sheet, in landscape mode, write your meeting objective. This serves as a guidepost as you sequence the rest of the storyboard. The remaining sheets will represent your slides. Label each one in landscape mode with a title at the top.

There are no hard-and-fast rules on the structure of your storyboard, and the exact slides you have will vary depending on the prospect and the potential partnership. One good rule of thumb is that if your meeting is one hour, you should have no more than ten slides (not including the title and table of contents) to allow time for introductions, a demo, and open dialogue through the meeting.

For a first meeting, this outline is a good starting point:

▸ **Meeting Title**

▸ **Table of Contents (a.k.a., "Topics for Today")**

▸ **Act One—Framing** *(do not write this on a slide; just write the below bullets on slides)*

- Who We Are (this one could be a slide or a round of introductions prior to presenting the slides)
- The State of the Ecosystem
- The Consumer Problem
- The [Your Company Name] Solution

▸ **Act Two—The Meat** *(do not write this on a slide; just write the below bullets on slides)*

- State of Your Business
- Demo
- Future Roadmap and Partnership Objectives

▸ **Act Three—The Ideas** *(do not write this on a slide; just write the below bullets on slides)*

- What We Can Do Together
- Partnership Phases for Discussion (one or two slides)
- Thank You and Next Steps

Now that you have a big-picture flow, you can start developing the content. Write down two to three bullet points of content for each slide. Then turn those bullet points into visuals for your slides.

Here are some core principles for turning your storyboard into a great presentation:

▸ **It's a story.** Use a hook and set context for your solution and how your two companies would be better together.

▸ **Stick to visuals.** Visuals are a memorable way to simplify and communicate complex concepts. The right picture can be worth more than a thousand words. It's important to explain the visuals, though, so create a "talk track" for each one. There are four informational diagrams that I often use in these sorts of presentations:

- *Hub and Spoke:* Picture a wheel with both companies in the hub. Each spoke branching out from the hub represents a partnership idea. Then the outer tire connects all the ideas into the larger partnering relationship. This helps you see the big picture of the entire partnership and also serves as a metaphor, where if you break a spoke or two, the wheel won't fall apart. Basically, the whole is greater than the sum of its parts.

- *Pizza (Pie Chart):* This visual can be used to show the relative importance of different partnership ideas. Each slice of pizza represents a partnership idea, with the size of the slice based on the strategic impact.

- *The Timeline:* This visual is an arrow from left to right starting with today and mapping out the milestones along the way to the significant goal that both companies cannot reach independently.

- *End Customer Journey:* In this visual, you present two flowcharts depicting the existing customer journey and the future customer journey, with an emphasis on how much the partnership could improve the customer experience. Put yourself in the end customer's shoes to identify the most impactful improvements.

▶ **Less is more.** When you first create your storyboard, don't worry about the length, or you might omit important information. I will often start with around fifteen slides to ensure I'm telling the full story. I then create an abridged version of five to seven slides (excluding the title, table of contents, and thank you/next steps slides) to zero in on the most important points. I move all the nonessential slides into the Appendix, so I still have the information if I need it.

▶ **Build the deck based on what your audience cares about.** Do your research and refer back to your P-SWOT. Each presentation should be highly tailored to your prospect.

▶ **Do not send slides out prior to meeting.** The slides are not meant to stand on their own. You want to tell the story around the slides to prevent misinterpretation and provide context. Sending the slides out ahead of time also steals your thunder and lessens the impact of presenting the slides and having the live discussion together. If you want to share the slides, always do so *after* the meeting. (The exception to this is your main prospect contact. You can share the slides with them to get feedback, especially if they're co-presenting with you.)

▶ **Slides are not your speaker notes.** Don't read bullet points directly from a slide. It's your job to make the meeting fun and engaging, with the attendees walking away saying, "That was the most productive meeting I've had all month," or something along those lines. Reading off a slide won't cut it.

▶ **Do a demo!** A demo helps to make the partnership concept more real and concrete. The specifics of the demo will vary depending on your company and the partnering idea. Perhaps you show a product sample, present a software integration, or talk through a "day in the life" of the end customer and demonstrate the product experience. Try to make it as relevant as possible to your audience, and if you're working with technology, plan to do a live demo but have a static demo backup plan.

Now that you know what you will discuss at the meeting, let's talk logistics to ensure things run smoothly.

LOGISTICS

Housekeeping for this initial meeting is a big deal. It can make or break your desired outcome at this point, which is to make a human connection, align that the partnership opportunity is too big to pass up, and agreed on the next actions. Prepare and manage what you can so there are no distractions. The rule of thumb here is to ensure that all meeting logistics are invisible to the meeting dialogue. Here are a few logistics to keep in mind.

▶ **Location, day, and time**

- Make it a face-to-face meeting. Make the trip to their office or host at your location. You won't have a second chance to make that first impression as a team, so make it count with an in-person human connection.

- Most internal meetings occur on Mondays and many people leave early on Fridays, so target Tuesday, Wednesday, or Thursday for the meeting. If Friday is the only availability, schedule in the first half of the day, and don't forget about potential time-zone differences.

- Don't be late. Be early! You want to start the meeting at the scheduled time, not be picked up in the lobby at the start time.

▶ **Attendees**

- Keep the first meeting small, with four or fewer attendees from both sides. The larger the meeting gets, the more formal it can be, not enabling enough open-air time for dialogue and discussion.

- Never outnumber your prospect's attendee number. Either have the same number or fewer.

- Balance out the titles and levels in the room. If you said the idea was your CEO's, they should be in the room for the meeting.

- Usually, the most senior person in the room from your company should do most of the talking, but depending on the topic, you and your executives can play off each other's points and dialogue.

▶ **Room size and setup**

- Get to know your contact's executive assistant. They are there to help you so that the meeting runs smoothly. Never forget to thank them after for making the meeting a success.

- Gather any info you can on the specific room with regards to size, configuration (table, chairs, sofas, etc.), and technical presentation setup. Is there a projector, or is it a TV? How large is the screen? What type of ports and cables does the tech use? HDMI? Something else? Are connection dongles or adapters provided in the room for your laptop type and for your demo devices? It's your job to prevent technical mishaps as you present.

- If the meeting is critical and not too far of a drive, I suggest going to the conference room and checking out the technical setup in person because some things are difficult to pre-check otherwise (e.g., what is the resolution of the TV or projector?) If a prior visit is not possible, then schedule an early arrival of thirty to forty-five minutes to get everything ready and have time to handle potential snags.

- Even if connection dongles are provided, always be prepared with your own adapters for every device you'll be using. It is your responsibility to pre-wire all setup so that your first meeting happens as smoothly as possible.

- Likewise, even if a presentation clicker is provided,

bring your own, since you know it works with your laptop and devices.

Okay, now that you have a slide deck and the logistics are out of the way, it's time for a dress rehearsal.

INTERNAL DRESS REHEARSAL

An internal dress rehearsal is one of the most important steps to ensure the meeting happens smoothly and successfully. The internal dress rehearsal should happen at least one to two weeks before the actual meeting with the prospect. Invite all the team members who will be in the partner meeting as well as their managers as optional attendees.

The internal prep meeting should have the following agenda:

▶ **Logistics of the upcoming meeting**

▶ **Objective of the partner meeting**

- Include the "why" here. Ensure that internal team members are aware of the potential value of a partnership with the prospect. Before the partner meeting, it is critical to have internal stakeholders on board, especially if they are responsible for any deliverables or talking points in the upcoming meeting. Also ensure they're on board with the potential outcome of the meeting.

- Be clear on the specific objective of the upcoming meeting in context of the overall partnership objective. Remember: this is just the beginning of an engagement, so the initial goal is to tee up the next meeting.

▶ **Who's who from the prospect team**

- Outline who is attending the upcoming meeting from the other company. Include their headshot, title, area of responsibility, and a bit about their background.

Also include info on other members of the prospect company that you or others in your company have been in contact with. It's helpful to use an org chart when presenting this information, so you can easily see the connections and different roles.

- Indicate which attendees are believers, which are neutrals, and which are skeptics (more on this in a bit).

▶ **What you know about the prospect's company**

- Get your internal team up to speed on the company and your competitive analysis of their business and strategy. Identify the gap that your company can fill ("what's in it for them") while also discussing the benefits to your company ("what's in it for us").

- Include latest happenings and news about the prospect's company, like challenges, new launches, recent executive hires, partnering and acquisition history, and so on.

▶ **Review the agenda and slide deck for the upcoming meeting**

- Walk through a draft of your slide deck. Include internal callouts (like digital post-it notes) on the slides to indicate if you need any internal support to work on the slide content.

- Assign roles for each of your team's attendees. Be clear about who will be talking throughout the meeting. Discuss and confirm who will be presenting each slide and where the handoffs will happen.

- Don't do too many handoffs, but plan to have a few so that your team can cover their domain areas. For example, whoever set up the meeting and organized it should kick off the meeting and be the orchestrator. The most senior person in the room should cover content about the company's vision and mission. A product leader can spearhead the demo and walkthrough of your solution. When doing the handoffs, simply hand your presentation clicker to the new presenter—make it easy and smooth.

- Do a dry run of the presentation, but don't rehearse word for word. You want the presentation to be natural and feel like a conversation, not a scripted hard sales pitch.

- When you practice, make sure you're using your "outside" voice. I don't mean the inside and outside voices we teach children, but the difference in how you speak inside your company and how you speak to people outside the company. Don't do the dress rehearsal like you're talking to your internal team members. Actually role-play the meeting. If you're going to switch to your "inside" voice, call it out—say, "I'm putting on my [company] hat." If you don't practice with your outside voice, you could easily slip up and use your inside voice in the meeting.

You are the conductor of this symphony, and all your prep will pay off in the meeting.

PREPARE FOR OPPOSITION: BELIEVERS, NEUTRALS, AND SKEPTICS

Part of your job is to offset any opposition in the meeting. The attendees from the other company will fall into one of three personas: believers, neutrals, or skeptics. Believers are advocates for a partnership with your company, neutrals are undecided, and skeptics are resistant to the idea. To prepare for potential issues that may come up in the face-to-face meeting, you need to understand *why* each person is either a believer, neutral, or skeptic.

Lay out the believers, neutrals, and skeptics in a table with their role and why they fall into a particular camp. It can look like this:

B/N/S	NAME, ROLE	WHY?
BELIEVER	JOHN LIVINGSTON, HEAD OF PARTNERSHIPS	Your main contact, helped build the ideas, knows his internal company challenges but is not sure yet how the partnership will be managed from concept to launch
NEUTRAL	ANDREW WAYNE, VP OPERATIONS	Open to new ideas at this point since he is managing a path to profitability and wants to get there faster
SKEPTIC	MARY LEVINE, VP ENGINEERING	Has an internal project already working with the same technology, built a team to work on it

Your objective is to turn the skeptics into believers. If you can do that, you will naturally win over the neutrals as well. Anticipate the opposition and what questions the other company's attendees could ask. The believers are already on board, so use them to help you convince the skeptics.

Turn skeptics into believers. This can take time, but stick with it. Create a simple "why" message to spread the word, get help from the believers, and prepare for potential opposition.

In the given example, John is a believer. He loves the ideas conceptually. He just needs to know who does what work to make it a reality in execution. He is your best sounding board to better understand what opposition could be faced in the meeting. After the meeting is set up, you can call a prep meeting between just you and him. Ask him directly about what questions and concerns are likely to come up in the meeting. Also ask him to co-present the ideas with you. You don't want any surprises, so send him a preview of the slide deck for the meeting and walk him through the slides so that he sees the plan and can provide feedback on the content and flow.

After your prep session with John, ensure your internal team also has clear roles and assigned talking points to address potential opposition. Role-play the conversations so you are all internally aligned on the answers. For example, Mary is our skeptic. She has an internal project already under way. She may feel like her solution is better, and she is likely worried she and her team could be replaced. So make sure you have your most technical person in the room to talk about the tech, how long the team has been working on it, and what you've learned along the way. Also discuss the ease of integration while pointing out that the prospect needs to do that work and that there will be ongoing management of the integration, to mitigate fears of replacement.

Don't forget about the neutrals. Andrew is looking at the situation objectively and thinking about how he can get his company profitable faster, so explain how the partnership will help accomplish those goals.

By taking time to understand the goals, worries, and hesitations of your audience, you can better address their oppositions and show them how your ideas will benefit them and their company.

PITCHING AND PARTNERING

The title of this chapter, "The Partnership Pitch," has two meanings. First, there's the obvious meaning: you are pitching the partnership. The second, less obvious meaning is that the pitch itself is a partnership. As you pitch, more than selling your ideas, what you're doing is having a conversation and building a relationship. You're basically getting a firsthand look at what a partnership would be like with this prospect.

Here's your checklist to complete before moving on to the next step:

▶ **Make it easy for your prospect to imagine a future together.** Help your prospect visualize what new value you can bring customers together by writing a personalized message.

▶ **Don't put all your eggs in one basket.** Get various irons in the fire and let them all heat up. Put *optionality* in effect, which is "the quality of being available to be chosen but not obligatory."

▶ **Really get to know your prospect and how their leadership team operates.** Get to know the culture through your partnership detective work. Understand what their CEO is most concerned about and who their competitors are. Find out about recent partnerships they have engaged in and how those engagements are evolving.

▶ **Build trust with prospects by taking turns peeling back one layer of the onion at a time.** Relationships are built on reciprocity. The more transparent you are, the more transparent your prospect will be (most of the time). But only share what you need to share that will benefit the partnership, and don't share everything all at once. Build the relationship over time, with several calls and meetings.

▶ **Turn skeptics into believers.** This can take time, but stick with it. Create a simple "why" message to spread the word, get help from the believers, and prepare for potential opposition.

At this point, you've painted the whole big picture, and you and your prospect are both leaning in. It's now time for the final part of aligning: formalizing the details of the partnership and closing the deal.

CHAPTER 10

FORMALIZING THE PARTNERSHIP AND DEAL

When I was with a connected device company, one of our big partnering strategies was to "go where the data flows," which meant bringing our devices to where new data was being created and consumed. Our goal was to move out of the computer accessory aisle, both in physical stores and online, and into the drone, VR, and gaming aisles. To that end, we were in a competitive situation to win a partnership deal with one of the top global video game console companies. The Big Idea was for us to create a branded connected device for their game console that would allow their end customers to store and play more games, as well as to use more controller types and charge them, with the broader goal of increasing playing time and further building brand affinity.

In general, you should always assume your prospect is considering other partners, but in this case, we actually got confirmation. While sharing his screen, one of our contacts accidentally showed his email inbox, revealing a request for proposal had been sent to our top competitor. At first, it felt like a gut punch, but ultimately, it was a good thing. When you know what you're up against, you can better prepare your proposal to prioritize and amplify the right areas of strength. I'd built a good relationship with my main contact at the company, so I openly asked him where he thought we stood out as a clear winner and where we may be falling short from their perspective. This helped me better understand how the competition was being perceived.

Our prospect was using our competitor as reference to evaluate us, so we had to create a competitive advantage for ourselves. We took several strategies to do so:

▸ **A better-together story:** Our competitor was providing a response to an RFP, so to stand out, we had to show our ability to think beyond the RFP, creating a better-together story that demonstrated our commitment to innovation and growth of the relationship. We outlined a 360-degree picture of the partnership and its scope with short, medium, and long views. We also backed our story up with hard data, sharing our successful experiences in selling similar devices with a drone company and a VR headset company.

▸ **A trusted relationship:** We approached the partnership from a place of great respect and recognition of our prospect's brand and products. That was actually one of the things that had first drawn us to the prospect. We wanted to work with high-caliber brands that had strong end consumer affinity. Mutual respect is always a good starting place, but it was especially important in this case because our prospect was based in another country. US-based companies can sometimes be perceived as too aggressive by certain cultures and in other parts of the world. By coming in humble, we showed them that we understood how important their brand values and principles were. We emphasized our commitment to preserving their brand identity and standard of quality, from product reliability and durability to speed and performance to design aesthetic.

▶ **A comprehensive proposal package:** Our proposal brought the potential collaboration to life with visual mock-ups of the branded devices in a variety of color choices, a timeline for a family of devices that we would bring to market as the game console itself evolved, details on the retail experience and packaging design for end consumers, a list of product features and technical specifications, and financial modeling with pricing (we set up a win-win deal structure, such that the more storage devices we sold, the more revenue our prospect generated as well). We also developed a physical, functional prototype using the prospect company's brand colors and logo. We even made a second prototype designed around one of the most popular game franchises. We demonstrated these live and in person with the prospect.

Ultimately, our hard work paid off, and we won the deal. The multi-year partnership is still going strong today.

Turning a prospect into a partner is a delicate process of negotiation and adaptation. The specific tactics will vary according to the prospect and partnership idea, but I'll share a few overarching tips and strategies to help guide you at this stage.

LEANING IN TOGETHER: PARTNERSHIP SCOPE

Assuming your pitch is successful, this is a major turning point in the partnership where you start leaning in together. Once you've gotten that initial yes from your prospect—meaning you have determined there should be a way to work together and both parties are open and transparent about feedback and input on ideas—you can create a key document together: the Partnership Scope document. This is a one-pager outlining the initial scope of the first "crawl" stage that serves as the test period of the partnership. If the "crawl" stage is only a path to get to the "walk" stage, then include both phases in this document. The "crawl" stage may be a necessary bridge but not be viewed as valuable enough to both parties on its own.

The Partnership Scope document should include the business model of the partnership. You've already been laying the foundation for the business model throughout the explore and align phases. Now you simply formalize it. What value will be created for you, your prospect, and the end consumer? Are there strong incentives? Is there a way to measure that success? How will the partnership be operated? The business model should be based on the Partnership Objectives and Principles (POP) document. Be sure to include the KPIs and metrics important to both companies.

In total, the Partnership Scope document should include:

▶ Partnership objectives

▶ Deliverables

▶ Roadmap (a high-level timeline with a launch target date at a minimum)

▶ The high-level roles and responsibilities for each party

▶ What assets you're bringing to the table and what assets your prospect is bringing to the table

▶ The North Star metric for you and for your partner (the

KPI or metric that will be used to measure the impact and success of this phase of the partnership)

Remember: this is a one-pager. This is a high-level outline of the partnership. Save the details for the term sheet and contract, which will come later. Right now, you're just putting some lines in the sand for what the initial scope is and what it is not.

Add a "Parking Lot" section at the end of the Partnership Scope document. This is where you can include additional ideas for the future. The objective of the "Parking Lot" is to ensure your prospect is aware of the items that are not in scope, to communicate how you're thinking about those ideas, and to assure all involved that you haven't missed anything.

SCENARIO PLANNING: WHAT MIGHT HAPPEN, AND HOW WILL YOU RESPOND?

When engaging prospects, theorizing decisions and planning for potential outcomes is important. You never know exactly what is going to happen, so I urge you and your internal team to do scenario planning to decide what you and your company should do based on how your prospect responds. It's also good to get other perspectives. After you've built out the scenarios, review them with your trusted internal stakeholders to align on not only the desired outcome but the process to get there.

A common tool for scenario planning is a decision tree. A decision tree is a flowchart of possible outcomes and consequences. It's a good way to visually see all the various decision points impacting the partnership, allowing you to map out the potential scenarios and organize workflows for how to respond.

The real trick to scenario planning, though, is not just knowing the potential outcomes but predicting which outcomes are most likely. *Game theory* can help you better predict what might happen, so you're less likely to be blindsided by your prospect's decisions and can also adjust the incentives and framing of your partnership proposal to influence decisions in the direction to benefit both parties and what's best for the partnership.

GAME THEORY

In simplified terms, game theory is the study of decision-making in situations in which there are varying interests and in which one participant's choices depend upon the choices of other participants. Even more simply, for partnerships, game theory is a way to think about how to make the best decisions possible for the relationship and while taking into account your prospect's or partner's potential decisions. Game theory challenges us to put ourselves in the shoes of the other "players" of the game and anticipate their possible actions and reactions. It is a way to play out various scenarios, predict what might happen, and plan our own decisions accordingly.

If you want an entertaining introduction to game theory, I recommend watching the movie *A Beautiful Mind*. It's a great movie that covers the life story of John Nash, who was a pioneering game theorist. For a less thrilling introduction, I'll go over some of the basics for you. First, in its purest form, game theory is the study of mathematical models, but don't worry: no advanced mathematics will be needed for our purposes. Originally, game theory addressed "zero-sum" games, in which each party's gains or losses are exactly balanced by those of the other parties. A zero-sum game is like slicing up a pizza. If you take a larger piece, someone else is going to get a smaller piece. There's only so much pizza, so the only way to get more is for someone else to get less. If the total gains of the parties are added up and the total losses are subtracted, they will sum to zero—hence the name, zero-sum game.

In contrast, a non-zero-sum scenario is where interacting participants' gains and losses can be more or less than zero. This is more relevant to partnerships. Remember when we talked about 1 + 1 = 3 (or more)? In win-win partnerships, both parties stand to gain. While a zero-sum game is competitive, non-zero-sum games can be collaborative.

The most well-known non-zero-sum game example is the Prisoner's Dilemma. In this thought experiment, two prisoners are captured by the police. The police suspect that the prisoners are responsible for a robbery, but they do not have enough evidence to prove it, though they are able to convict the prisoners of a lesser charge, with a sentence of one year in jail. The prisoners are put in separate cells with no way to communicate with one another. Each is offered a deal: if they testify against their accomplice, they get immunity, and their accomplice will be sentence to ten years. If both testify against the other, they will both be held responsible and sentenced to five years each. If neither prisoner confesses, both will be convicted of the lesser offense and sentenced to one year.

We can visualize the possible outcomes with a payoff matrix:

PRISONER 2

		TESTIFIES	STAYS SILENT
PRISONER 1	**TESTIFIES**	5, 5	0, 10
	STAYS SILENT	10, 0	1, 1

Let's think like Prisoner 1. Of course we're looking to minimize our prison time. We have no way of knowing if Prisoner 2 has testified against us. Let's first assume that he has not. If we don't testify either, we both will go to prison for one year. Not a bad outcome. But if we testify, we go free, while Prisoner 2 gets ten years. Let's assume there is no honor system here and each prisoner only cares about themselves and serving less time. In that case, if Prisoner 2 does not testify, we'll be better off if we do. The other possibility is that Prisoner 2 does testify. In that case, if we do not testify as well, we go to jail for ten years, but if we do testify, we get only five years. It's clearly better to testify in this case as well.

It's clear that the best payoff for both prisoners is when neither testifies. But game theory advocates that both should testify. Since you have no way of influencing the other player's decision, no matter what he does, you're better off testifying. But on the other hand, you're both in the same situation. Both of you should be sensible enough to realize that testifying undermines the best outcome for both players. There is no single *right* solution to the Prisoner's Dilemma, and that's why it's a dilemma.

We can generalize this game scenario to any two-party situation in which the best all-around outcome is for both to cooperate but the worst individual outcome is to be a cooperating player while the other player defects.

Okay, now that we have the basics of game theory under our belt, let's apply this to partnership decision-making.

GAME THEORY IN CO-ELEVATE PARTNERSHIPS

For this example, we'll use the mattress industry, which is going through a massive transition, with the established players like Simmons and Tempur Sealy being challenged by the likes of Purple and Casper. We're seeing this kind of digital disruption, with large physical retailers being threatened by digital-first e-tailers, across many verticals today.

Let's say you're leading partnerships for Fullpower, an AI-based company that analyzes personalized sleep and snoring patterns, with coaching and automatic responses to snoring. Fullpower's mission is to radically improve customers' sleep experiences through continued innovation. As part of this mission, Fullpower wants to provide customers with a smart bed. For example, when the Fullpower platform detects snoring, the bed could raise and elevate the upper body fifteen degrees to minimize snoring. Then a sleep report and sleep score would be emailed each morning with heart and breathing rates along with sleep coaching for the user to get a better night's sleep. To build their own smart bed, Fullpower would need a lot of resources and skill sets it doesn't currently have, and it could take up to five years. Similarly, if a major mattress company tried to create their own smart bed, they would face gaps of talent, and it would probably take them about four years. So your Big Idea is to partner with a mattress company, integrating your technology with existing beds and leveraging their brand and distribution network, in order to bring a smart bed to market in just one year.

You approach the CEO of Tempur Sealy with your partnership concept, including a few use cases and customer scenarios. You outline your perspective of the market and how it's evolving, emphasizing the market challenges to established players. With the Fullpower technology platform, they can push their offerings to another level in a short period of time and greatly increase their value to consumers in the market. By providing unique innovations that the other guys don't, Tempur Sealy can continue to differentiate their offering beyond a low-price knife fight (metaphorical, of course) and justify their top-of-the-market pricing.

If Tempur Sealy partners with you, they will advance their launch of a smart bed by three years, and you will advance your launch by four years. Now, if Tempur Sealy doesn't want to partner with you, you may go partner with another mattress company instead. Or if you decide not to partner with Tempur Sealy, they may go partner with a different technology company.

So let's look at a payoff matrix for this scenario, with the numbers representing the years to initial launch:

		FULLPOWER	
		PARTNERS	DOESN'T PARTNER
TEMPUR SEALY	PARTNERS	1, 1	1, 4
	DOESN'T PARTNER	3, 1	3, 4

Now, this is obviously simplified. You can add more variables. For example, maybe if Tempur Sealy partners with a different technology company, it will take two years to create the smart bed instead of one, or it will have fewer features. Or if they develop the tech in-house, they might risk quality issues. They also risk a competitor gaining a head start. If you partner with a different mattress company, perhaps you'll get a smaller distribution network or less brand recognition to use. When possible, try to make your payoff matrix quantitative, but you can also add qualitative notes. Use the payoff matrix to find all the related deal points you and your prospect have in the negotiations.

There's also one very big difference between a partnership scenario and the Prisoners' Dilemma: you and your prospect can talk to each other! You can get a sense of the direction they're leaning, tailor your negotiations based on the deal points, and highlight how the best option for both of you is to partner.

This simplified framework can then help you plan for the various scenarios and how the parties may be evaluating the paths forward with a partnership.

PARTNERSHIP SCENARIO PLANNING: WHAT DO YOU DO WHEN THERE ARE FORKS IN THE ROAD?

As part of your scenario planning, also think about the decisions to make down the road after an initial agreement with a partner. There will be new competitors and new innovations, and you must get ahead of these decision points so that you and your partner know what you will do when you're faced with a crossroads. Those future crossroads can be outlined in the form of *partnership scenario planning*, which is the exercise of outlining a few paths for the future of the partnership.

The specific scenarios can be very unique to your business and your partner's business. For example, maybe your business has long-term plans to transition to a new online shopping platform. How might that affect the partnership? There are also general scenarios to think through. For example, will the partnership be an exclusive agreement, or will you or your partner be forming similar partnerships with others? Will the partnership expand into other business units within your companies? Could the partnership lead to a joint venture or consideration for acquisition?

Partnership scenario planning is best done as a one-on-one session with your main partner contact. Make sure to do this exercise only after you both have a clear understanding as well as buy-in on the initial phase of your partnership. The way to present this session to your contact is to say that you want to ensure that the partnership is for the long term and will withstand change over time.

CREATING URGENCY TOGETHER

Even when you have an equal value partnership concept and a strong partnership business case, getting both organizations to prioritize and to move forward with the partnership effort can still be challenging. To close the deal, there needs to be a sense of urgency on both sides and equal motivation to move forward. FOMO, FUD, and scarcity/abundance are ways to emphasize the urgency.

FOMO is "fear of missing out." One of the biggest motivators is the idea that if we don't move forward now, we will miss out on the opportunity. You can tap into FOMO by being transparent about any parallel conversations you're having with other companies. All communication must be honest and relevant, so don't make stuff up about who else you are talking to. But if your prospect really could miss out on the opportunity, they deserve to know, so they can make the best, most informed decision for their company.

FUD stands for "fear, uncertainty, and doubt." Especially if you're a small company, considering FUD can be a strategy. Build FUD based on factual information about your prospect's market area: Where is it now, and where is it going? Avoid misusing FUD to influence perception by disseminating over-ly negative or false information. The objective is to communi-cate factual market intelligence that your prospect may not be aware of but should be.

Scarcity and abundance are about how you view the availabil-ity of resources (or, in this case, opportunities). An abundance mindset, in the context of a partnership, is the belief that there is enough financial and strategic success in the relationship for all parties, even without the comprehensive quantitative analysis in front of you. It is the optimistic perspective of what is possi-ble. A scarcity mindset is the belief that resources are limited, which causes fixation on short-term coping versus longer-term problem-solving, causing more relationship stress and lack of partnership confidence. Thanks to Stephen Covey, author of *The 7 Habits of Highly Effective People*, for the scarcity and abun-dance mindset concepts.

In partnerships, when creating the relationship, you want to evoke an abundance mindset. When you have a specific oppor-tunity to act on that you want to create urgency around, evoke a scarcity mindset. A way to do this is to have a defined timeline and to mention alternatives being evaluated. You can say some-thing like this based on facts, "We are seeking out the one right partner in the next thirty days to go after this market opportunity together. While other alternatives may exist, given our existing relationship, we want to give our team the chance to explore the possibilities together and build on a long-standing partnership." I call this *framing the concept*. Instead of just outlining the idea, you frame it in terms of the prospect and the timing. The fram-ing addresses "why them" and "why now." "Why them" is based not on their business strengths but on the relationship and trust. "Why now" creates a timeline based on a milestone with ele-ments of scarcity and alternatives (other companies to engage).

Creating a sense of urgency in these ways is not meant to be a manipulation. Rather, it is a way to convey the reality and time constraints of the situation so that you can get a faster decision, allowing both you and your partner to start realizing outcomes and rewards of the partnership.

NAVIGATING MULTIPLE PARTNERSHIPS

Back in the 2000s, I was working for an internet media company. At that time, there was a big push to develop new experiences on devices outside of a computer and web browser. Specifically, I was part of an initiative to bring internet experiences to televisions. We were trying to create the first mass-market smart TVs.

We first designed what the customer experience could look like on a TV, independent of what was technically feasible. Then we engaged a TV manufacturer to share our idea and vision. As part of the partnership exploration, our prospect provided us with a TV prototype that had an RJ45 port (internet jack). This allowed our engineering team to develop our own prototype. It was rudimentary and far from the vision we'd outlined, but we knew we were on to something. A user could navigate and engage with internet applications on a television for the first time ever—it was a breakthrough!

While we were working with this prospect, we started to see that other TV manufacturers were also including internet access on their new prototypes, mostly for TV firmware updates at the time. So we started to engage with other prospects. Over the next year, there was massive pressure on our team to deliver the technology and customer experiences. In parallel, the BD team and I were drumming up new partnerships, which was challenging in its own right, as each partner was completely different, from company culture to decision-making. We ended up with four partners.

After months and months of hard work, our team vision and dream became reality at CES (Consumer Electronics Show). All four of our partners presented the TVs we had developed together. We ended up winning a Best in Show award, which was a tremendous accomplishment.

Would it surprise you to learn that this experience contains some of my biggest lessons learned from my career? CES was a huge win for my company. We were able to come out and make a big industry bang. Our partners, though, were less happy. We had not informed them we were working with others in the industry. They were trying to differentiate and thought we were helping them to do that, when in reality we'd provided a similar experience to all of the big players. Our partners were understandably angry with us. One of them stopped working with our company for many years because of it.

This kind of thing can negatively impact not just your company but also you as an individual. Later, when I had moved to a different company, I needed to work with TV manufacturers again, and the CEO of one of the companies said, "I've worked with Rich before, and I'm not sure I can trust him." That was a huge soul-searching moment for me. He wasn't being a jerk; he was just being honest. At the internet media company, I wasn't the one calling the shots, but now I was, and I wanted to do things differently. I asked the CEO to give me a chance to prove myself. It took time and work, but I was able to build back the trust I'd lost, and we formed a successful win-win partnership together. Fast-forward another few years, and I was at a start-up and had a new opportunity to partner with this TV manufacturer. This time, because of the goodwill I'd built, they were thrilled to partner with me again, and they became the start-up's very first partner.

I was very lucky to get a second chance. That's not always the case, so you need to be thoughtful the first time around.

When engaging multiple prospects, be very careful with con text switching. It's far easier than you'd expect to put the wrong logo on a slide or slip up and say the wrong thing in a meeting. Once, while I was in a meeting with one prospect, I had a calendar invite pop up from another prospect. It only takes one slip, and then the cat's out of the bag. Always, always, *always* be very careful about the information you share during meetings.

Just as you might be engaging multiple companies, your prospect may also be considering multiple partners. Some prospects may be open to sharing who else is in the partner-selection process, but beware of this level of transparency. While being open is good to gather intel for your own proposal, keep in mind that if they're sharing this level of information with you, they are likely sharing the same information with the other companies. It's good to address confidentiality early on (more on this in the next section).

As you move into partnership, I encourage more transparency (within reason). For example, if I had a do-over for the smart TV example, I would tell the TV manufacturers that we were working with others, though I probably couldn't share specific details. Then I would either find ways to provide unique features for each or perhaps launch with only one partner in the short term, with some exchange for that exclusivity.

If you're new to partnerships, it's better to focus your energies on a single partnership. One partner will open the door to other partners. If you have partnering experience, you can do simultaneous partnerships, but be careful to not damage any of your relationships.

> **Pursue select prospects but have one lead partnership.** One partner will open the door to other partners. Your first partner will help to form your mindset on the ecosystem and determine when and how you approach the next partner.

So, yes, get multiple irons in the fire and keep them warm, but treat each prospect with respect and maintain trust. You never know when you'll want to partner with them in the future.

ELEPHANTS IN THE ROOM: CONFIDENTIALITY AND IP

When it comes to partnering, you need to navigate your prospect company's politics as well as your own company's. Company culture often inhibits a willingness to collaborate. According to a Forbes Insights survey, 50 percent of executives say their company's culture—specifically, a "pride in ownership" mentality or "not invented here" syndrome—prevents better collaboration with partners. The big elephants in the room are concern over intellectual property (IP) and confidentiality.

In practice, ownership and protection of IP can become one of the greatest obstacles for a company to work more intimately with others. It's essential for partnerships and BD professionals to fully understand context and concepts related to IP, as this domain can either unlock new levels of collaboration and value for both parties or become the worst nightmare for a partnership. The good news is the risks surrounding IP are manageable.

In partnerships, especially those involving product and technology development, there are generally four types of IP and knowledge assets, as defined by Professors Ove Granstrand and Marcus Holgersson:

▶ **Background IP/knowledge:** IP/knowledge that is relevant to a collaborative venture or open innovation project that is supplied by the partners at the start of the project

▶ **Foreground IP/knowledge:** IP/knowledge that is produced within the collaborative venture or open innovation project during the project's tenure

▶ **Sideground IP/knowledge:** IP/knowledge that is relevant to a collaborative venture or open innovation project but produced outside the project by any of the partners during the project's tenure

▶ **Postground IP/knowledge:** IP/knowledge that is relevant to a collaborative venture or open innovation project that is produced by any of the partners after the project ends

These IP topics need to be proactively discussed and agreed upon before formally establishing the partnership. A full legal breakdown goes beyond the scope of this book, but as some general guidance, start by building a close, trusted relationship internally with your legal team. Consult your legal counsel before any discussion with the prospect related to IP. They can advise you how best to label documents for sharing and how to handle emails with the prospect and internal communications on the partnership and deal.

As you introduce and discuss engagement scenarios as well as ownership and sharing guidelines for the partnership, ensure your prospect understands the four types of IP. For more complex issues, be certain to address what happens with any new IP that may arise within the collaboration. Create language with your legal team to support a relationship where whatever is your prospect's remains your prospect's, whatever is yours remains yours, and whatever you codevelop is shared. That is, unless some specific payment for research changes hands. In that case, if you fund it, it can be yours (depending on the terms), and vice versa.

On the confidentiality side, nondisclosure agreements (NDAs) are fundamental. Share with the prospect early on that confidentiality is important as you build a relationship and partnership, and explain that an NDA is critical for your companies to be able to align across teams. This sends a dual message that you are treating the information they share with the upmost confidentiality and that the information you share should be treated with the same amount of prudence.

In some cases, your legal counsel may advise you to put a project-specific NDA in place beyond a company-to-company NDA. The project-specific NDA will likely outline the initiative area and may include a named list of the team, with roles and employee names. This level of protection may be worth the upfront time and effort, but be careful not to lose too much time in the legal process or taint your company's ability to collaborate early on. At the same time, don't compromise your confidentially needs or your prospect's. Again, your legal counsel is your best friend here. You may also want to establish a project or initiative code name. This code name can be a fun yet essential way to protect confidentiality early on and throughout a deal execution process. Keep the code name simple, and develop it with your prospect to make it a trust and relationship builder.

It is paramount that your company's working team for the partnership project is aware of how important confidentiality is of your assets, processes, and IP. Ensure they have a clear understanding of the legal guidelines related to the partnership scope. Interpret those guidelines and make them easy to understand and have practical use for the team. Give examples of what the internal team can and cannot share with the new partner. Role-play scenarios of sample questions that could be asked by the partner. In general, if a member of the working team is uncomfortable with answering a question from a partner or doesn't know the answer, it's okay and best to say, "I don't know the answer to that," and refer to the overall partnership lead. It is important to set these rules of engagement with the partner and the working team on the partnership initiative so that everyone knows what to expect.

NEGOTIATION: FROM BIG IDEAS TO COMMITTED INITIATIVES

As you gain alignment with your prospect on the Partnership Scope document, you can begin the process of legally documenting the agreement. That starts with a term sheet and negotiation, leading to a contractual commitment by both parties.

A term sheet is a summary of the terms and conditions of the tentative business agreement. Your Partnership Scope document forms the foundation for the term sheet. The term sheet is usually formatted starting with bullet points, and it helps to get all parties literally on the same page. Make sure that the expectations and timelines set by BD are realistic and committed to by the other functions in the organization that will actually carry out the work. Depending on your level of experience with legal business documents, it's best to work closely with your legal team on this. While the term sheet is not itself a legally binding document, it will serve as a template for a more detailed legal contract. Lean in and don't underestimate the time and effort required to finalize the contractual terms.

> **It's not real until the ink dries (or until the electronic signature is submitted).** Become good friends with your legal counsel, as you'll be in the trenches with them to dot every i and cross every t in the agreement. Stay true to the Partnership Scope and vision that you've already aligned on.

If you have a clear understanding of what the partnership will involve and align expectations with your prospective partner, you may just build a relationship that lasts. You will likely need to do some negotiating first, though. Every negotiation is unique, and there are several steps in the contract and negotiation process that I don't have the space to cover here—the art of negotiation may need to be another book someday! For now, I'll give a broad overview.

The most important thing in negotiating is to deeply understand the key deal points and know your negotiation boundaries. Prior to negotiating business terms, understand what is most important to your company in relation to the deal and partnership. Also understand what is most important to your prospect. These are the key deal points, and they serve as the basis to developing the right business deal structure that both parties can align on. The wrong terms or a lack of understanding of the objectives can kill the deal, as you and your prospect may feel you're too far apart on terms and are not getting enough value out of the partnership. Ideally, you will be building on the work you've already done and will be aligned on the objectives and purpose of the deal and partnership.

Bend but don't break. The goal is to be like bamboo throughout negotiation, flexible where you can be and firm where it matters.

Then start laying out the terms. Each term should correspond with the mechanics of how the partnership will operate. For example, what are the specifics of the product or service being created, and how will both parties contribute to the offering? How will the offering be sold to customers? How will revenue and profits be shared? How will reporting and data sharing work? How will you handle future joint planning?

Assuming you do agree on a term sheet, then with the help of your legal team, you can draw up a contract.

For each term, know your negotiation boundaries. Go back to your scenario planning to think through what might come up in negotiation, and determine your "floor" or "ceiling" for each major term. Understand where you're willing to compromise and where you're not.

Try to continually gauge the level of interest so that you're not blindsided and can either get ahead of any issues or walk away before sinking too much time into the engagement. Everything is a learning experience that you can use to improve future pitches and negotiations.

Learn and move on. Not every prospect will turn into a partner, and that's okay. Don't get too hung up if you get a no. Seek to understand why a prospect said no, and then move on.

Beware of negotiation fatigue which sets in when you and your prospect have tried multiple ways to address key deal points but unable to close the gaps with agreement. You may have reached an impasse and come to a conclusion. On the other hand, you've been able to develop creative ways to meet your prospect's objectives and yours, without making compromises, you have win-win deal ready for signature.

ANNOUNCE AND SOCIALIZE

After closing the contract, it's time to share more about the new partnership internally. It should be no surprise to the leadership team of your company that the contract is completed, but the scope of the partnership will not be totally clear to the broader team. Identify the right forum post-contract to introduce the partnership to the broader internal team or to the entire company, depending on the impact and scope of the agreement.

If there is going to be an external press release announcing the partnership, you can send an internal email just prior to the press release. Indicate that a press release will be coming out announcing the new partnership and that you and the leadership team are excited about the journey that your company and the new partner will be embarking on. Highlight what the partnership means to your company, tying it back to the company's core mission and objectives.

If this new partnership has long-term, strategic potential or if there are many internal skeptics, take this opportunity to further socialize the partnership inside of your company. A great forum may be an all-hands meeting where you allocate time for an update about the new partnership. It can be effective to present that update with your main partner contact, especially if there's still internal skepticism.

> **Let your partner do the talking.** Your partner contact knows their company and product way better than you. Get them onto your company turf to explain why the partnership matters to them and even do a demo.

You and your partner contact can kick things off together and discuss the power of the partnership and why both companies are venturing along that path. Then your partner contact can share more about their company, culture, and future ahead. End the presentation together and thank your partner contact and their company for the relationship while looking forward to the partnership now and in the future.

OFFICIALLY PARTNERS!

Closing the deal is the culmination of hours upon hours of hard work. It is a major milestone in making your Big Idea a reality. Take a moment to celebrate with your partner.

Here are your key takeaways:

▶ **Pursue select prospects but have one lead partnership.** One partner will open the door to other partners. Your first partner will help to form your mindset on the ecosystem and determine when and how you approach the next partner.

▶ **It's not real until the ink dries (or until the electronic signature is submitted).** Become good friends with your legal counsel, as you'll be in the trenches with them to dot every i and cross every t in the agreement. Stay true to the Partnership Scope and vision that you've already aligned on.

▸ **Bend but don't break.** The goal is to be like bamboo throughout negotiation, flexible where you can be and firm where it matters.

▸ **Learn and move on.** Not every prospect will turn into a partner, and that's okay. Don't get too hung up if you get a no. Seek to understand why a prospect said no, and then move on.

▸ **Let your partner do the talking.** Your partner contact knows their company and product way better than you. Get them onto your company turf to explain why the partnership matters to them and even do a demo.

After all this hard work to assess and identify the right partner, engage the prospect, and close the deal, the last thing you want is for the partnership to fail to meet expectations in execution. It's time to discuss how you can create a solid, effective partnership for the long haul.

STAGE 3

EXECUTE: GAINING ALTITUDE

CHAPTER 11

FROM PROSPECT TO PARTNER

I was in a major bind. I was working for a Fortune 500 video streaming company, and I was responsible for our partnership with a top consumer electronics company based in Japan. We were on a strict timeline to make our streaming service work at the quality levels needed to function on the next year's TVs from our partner. We had hit a major issue in the process, a launch-gating software bug that could not be fixed without hardware changes on the TVs. My company couldn't do anything about it; it was something our partner had to change. The challenge was that our partner had already completed multiple testing cycles for all the hardware of the next year's TVs. My main contact explained that there was a different internal team responsible for the hardware specification, and they couldn't make the changes we needed.

"What would it take for your partner contact to make the change required?" I asked.

"At this point, nothing. That ship has sailed."

We were at an impasse. In about one week, the TV hardware was going to be locked down, and no further changes could be made to them. At this point in time, my company's software enabling our streaming service was not going to be available on millions of TVs the next year, which would obviously be a huge issue. We were running out of options. I set up a last-ditch call with the partner contact for the next day.

I got together with my main engineer, who was originally from Japan, so he was completely in tune culturally and with the language. As an added bonus, he had previously worked at this partner company. Before my engineer and I got on the call, we planned out our approach and the outcome we were trying to achieve. We knew we were not going to solve the issue on the phone, but we could try to build trust and credibility with this partner contact. Together, we created a document with visuals so both teams had something to refer to throughout the phone meeting.

Having my engineer on the call went a long way. For one, it allowed us to have the discussion in Japanese with a few breaks for translation without slowing the conversation down. On the call, we recognized and acknowledged the issue and how hard it was to change. We shared a few ideas and options that opened up the discussion further and got our partner more engaged in the problem-solving.

Toward the end of the call, I paused the conversation to mention a risky but planned part of the conversation: I was going to ask for us to meet in person, even though it was last minute and could be seen as pushy. "This partnership is very important to our company, and we will do whatever it takes to support you in this situation. We want to work with you as one team to further discuss these ideas since it sounds like we are making some progress. If we find a solution together that can work for you, great. But if not, that's okay too. At least we will know we tried our best together to remedy the situation. While we made progress over the phone today, I feel that we can collaborate most effectively in person. If it's okay with you, can we continue the conversation in Tokyo tomorrow?" If I had proposed this too soon, they would have shut it down immediately. At this point, though, we had opened up enough of a window of hope that our partner contacts had started to see a "maybe" solution out there. We just needed to work further together to lock it in ASAP.

They agreed to the plan, so my engineer and I were on a plane to Tokyo the next day. After an eleven-hour flight, we sat down for the face-to-face meeting with the partner. We focused on our shared goal. Both companies had already made the decision to make my company's streaming service available on the partner's TVs, so the question was: How do we ensure that the user experience is high quality enough to meet both of our standards?

About halfway through the meeting, we found an opening for compromise. We would limit a feature in our software for a short period of time until our partner could make an update, and they would make what they called a "running change" on their hardware assembly line. My company's service was included on their TVs that year, enabled by changes they had never made before.

It was one of the most satisfying experiences I've had in my career—not just because of the outcome, but also because of the process. I'm proud of how both teams came together to create a solution and plan that worked for both companies. We kept the dialogue collaborative, and we started brainstorming and making decisions together. With us being in the room versus on the phone, our hardware partner contact felt more obligated and accountable to create some solutions. We both wanted the same outcome, but we also both needed to bend to agree on a solution ... and we did!

Once a prospect becomes a partner, the next stage of real work begins. The partnership is official in theory and on paper, but it's now time to engage the working teams and start executing to make it a reality. In one of my past lives, in addition to a BD leader, I was a partner program manager, and my sole responsibility was to build and manage partner projects across various internal teams. It is a really hard job. As I mentioned early in the book, creating a Co-Elevate Partnership is like building an entirely new virtual company. In the process of building this company and gaining altitude, things may get bumpy. In this chapter we'll cover how to more successfully establish, manage, and grow a strategic partnership.

HOW ARE BUSINESS PARTNERSHIPS SIMILAR TO PERSONAL RELATIONSHIPS?

My biggest tip is to remember that a partnership is a relationship. Now, of course, business partnerships are not about finding your soulmate, but just like partnerships, marriages are about building lifelong relationships. Learning the secrets to successful personal relationships can help you be a better business partner as well. As with many things in life, I turned to Oprah for insight about successful personal relationships ☺. Oprah Daily published a great article titled "The Secret to Having a Happy Marriage." It gave me not only valuable advice for my personal married life but also a new lens through which to view business partnerships. Drawing from this article and insights from my own experiences, here are the key principles for successful partner relationships.

EVEN HAPPY PARTNERS ARGUE

Conflict and tension in a business partnership is not a bad thing. It's all about how you handle the situation. When I see and hear something that I know is not right in a partnership, I stop, figure out why it's a red flag to me, and address it. If we don't call out the red flags, the foundation of the partnership won't be strong enough to last.

When conflicts arise, pre-wire and plan internally, so that your team is aligned on what you're trying to accomplish, and then follow this simple three-step process:

1. Understand and recognize what matters most. Get clear on the issues and why they matter, and place them in context by emphasizing the longer-term, broader relationship. In the big picture, what is most important?

2. Find and acknowledge the common ground. Instead of having one company versus the other, reframe the discussion as "us" versus "them" or the problem. Bring the conversation back to the joint purpose of why you're both partnering in the first place: the win-win Big Idea.

3. Work as one team to solve the issue. Don't take "no" as the final answer, and get creative. There are always other options if you're working collaboratively and thinking longer term. Maybe you make a short-term compromise with an agreement to address the challenges at a committed later date.

As you work through conflicts, make sure to leave egos out of it. While you want to find a solution, control your eagerness and beware of being perceived as desperate or applying too much pressure on the partner. Express that you're simply exploring possible solutions, and if you're unable to find one, you're okay to not move forward. Not all conflicts can be solved, and it's okay to walk away if you reach an impasse and can't find a resolution. Stay objective and don't make it personal. Sometimes, that's the best way to preserve the relationship for future partnering opportunities.

DON'T UNDERESTIMATE THE POWER OF HUMAN CONNECTION

Take the time to get to know your partner contacts on a personal level. What gets them out of bed in the morning for the job, and what are their passions outside of work?

Face-to-face time will strengthen the connection. In strategic partnerships, especially when there are challenges to work through, like in the opening story, in-person collaboration is essential. I know we've all become videoconference experts and many of us work remotely, but strategic partnerships frequently involve uncharted territory and situations where face-to-face human connection is necessary for real-time problem-solving and trust-building. So don't hesitate to ask for an in-person meeting (but be prepared to travel to your partner). Also plan for some non-meeting time together, like breakfast, dinner, or so on, to form a stronger bond.

You will naturally "click" with some people more than others. That's okay. You don't need to be best friends with every partner contact, but you do need to treat each other with respect. To me, a big part of being respectful is understanding and operating within your partner's culture. The more you do this, the easier you make their job. Familiarize yourself with both their company culture and their regional culture. If you have an internal contact who is from the region, they can serve as your cultural bridge and perhaps your translator as well, if language is a barrier. Collaborating in the partner's language and how they do business not only shows respect and builds trust but also helps discussions run more smoothly.

It's easy to maintain a human connection when things are going well. It can be more challenging when things go wrong. Tempers can run hot during partnerships, and things can get emotional. I've had people treat me with blatant disrespect and even yell profanity at me. In these situations, beware of tit for tat. This is when one party responds with an equivalent in return. Don't play this game. From my experience, it almost always results in a downward trend, damaging the relationship. If you've been insulted or your partner has done something out of line or unacceptable from your perspective, take a Zen approach. You can't control what they do, but you can choose how you respond. Keep your composure, and don't take it personally. Take a breather if needed. Physically leave the situation and go for a walk.

Note that this does not mean being a pushover. Keep the engagement professional and be kind, but hold on to your principles and the objectives of the partnership. You will sometimes encounter people who are aggressive, especially in negotiations. You can't be intimidated. Try to mirror them, bringing a similar energy. But always remember that you're representing your company. Keep it highly professional while being clear about your boundaries.

APPRECIATE EACH OTHER

Co-Elevate Partnerships are often built over many months or years. Basically, they're a marathon, not a sprint. When first starting a partnership, it's easy to be excited and appreciative. Over time, we can get lost in the day-to-day work. Maybe your partner contact isn't as organized as you, or their company's marketing isn't as polished as you'd like, or their team doesn't have the same technical skills as yours. But I bet they do some things *better* than you too. Instead of getting frustrated by your partner's weaknesses, focus on their strengths. That's why you started this partnership in the first place.

Understand and use the strengths each partner brings to the virtual partnership company. Creating a partnership is like creating a new company. Each partner should use each other's strengths as much as possible, including brand and marketing budget, to ensure the partnership is a success.

Acknowledge and be grateful for your partner. If they take time out of their busy day to speak to you, if they always meet their deadlines, if they keep a cool head during conflicts, let them know you appreciate it. And be sure to celebrate the smaller milestones together as you work toward your big goal.

ACCEPT AND EXPECT CHANGE

Look, I wrote a whole book about partnerships—obviously I think they're important. But a single partnership is not going to solve all of your or your company's be-all and end-all. Partnering is one piece in the larger puzzle of success. Give each partnership the time and care it requires, but don't rely on it too much, or it will lead to an unhealthy relationship dynamic where you cannot accommodate change. Change is the only constant in this world, so your company and your career need to be bigger than any one partnership.

Company goals may shift, the market and industry could evolve through new innovations, or customer behaviors and expectations may change. Any number of internal or external business, product, and technology factors can cause companies to rethink a partnership's value and terms. Partnerships will naturally evolve and change over time. Sometimes they may end, but they can also grow into bigger and better things. And even when a partnership does end, it can open the door for new opportunities. So be prepared for and open to change.

PARTNERSHIP KICKOFF: OPERATIONALIZING THE VIRTUAL PARTNERSHIP ORGANIZATION

Besides establishing a strong relationship, the most important key to a successful partnership is to have a good, clearly communicated structure and process. As a deal transitions to an active partnership, the project must be operationalized in order to execute the agreed-upon plan. We are moving from hunting to gathering, which means we need a different skill set. It's time for the BD manager to hand the reins over to the copilot, the partner manager who will be responsible for the overall relationship health with the partner as well as maybe growing the partnership value and scope over time. Or if the same person is performing both roles, it's time for them to put on a new hat and focus on execution of the partnership deal.

Once the partnership agreement is signed, ensure there is a partner manager assigned to the partnership as a whole, not just the specific project or the Phase 1 launch. To ensure a smooth transition, this assignment should be in place at least thirty days prior to the agreement being signed. It's best to approach leadership of the partner management team about the deal when it is in process and the business terms are being negotiated, so they can provide input. If there is no headcount designated for the partnership post-deal, it is time to secure those resources. Make sure the partner manager understands the key terms of the deal with regards to scope of work, timing and any schedule expectations, and responsibility of activities (who is doing what) throughout the length of the agreement.

The partner manager (let's assume that's you) should then set a date for the partnership kickoff session, which will be the initial meeting between the two teams to discuss and plan for the execution of the work. Give yourself at least two to three weeks to prep for this critical meeting. Determine your counterpart at the partner company who will be your main single point of contact (SPOC) on a daily basis throughout the development of the partnership. Set up a prep call or face-to-face meeting (if possible) between you and the main SPOC to cover the following key topics that you will discuss with the broader team in the partnership kickoff session.

WHO DOES WHAT?

The first task is to clearly define the core team from both companies that will be working on the partnership. The Partnership Scope document will give you a good idea of what needs to be done, so you can determine who needs to be involved.

Determine the functional leads from both companies, these leads may differ from the leads in stages prior to completing the deal. For example, who will be technical and engineering leads for the project? Who will lead product, marketing, security, QA, and any other main functions that need representation in the project?

Even though you are the SPOC on the project, a partnership is not managed just by a partner manager. A partnership is managed by anyone that has communication with that partner. So your goal is to connect the right contacts from both companies. You and your SPOC counterpart will serve as the escalation points and quarterbacks for the combined partnership team.

HOW WILL YOU MEASURE SUCCESS?

You've already done a lot of work figuring out the KPIs and your companies' North Star metrics. Now you can dig into the details of how you will measure and track success, which will help you continue to refine your forecasting of the partnership's business impact and keep a pulse on its progress. The Partnership Objectives and Principles (POP) document is a valuable resource here. Which metrics you use depend on the partnership, but let's run through some common metrics you might want to consider tracking.

If you're driving a user acquisition metric, start with the total audience that your prospect has engaged to determine the overlap with your company's (or initiative's) total *addressable audience*. Of that total addressable audience, how many users will become *aware* of your product or service based on the integration scope of the partnership? Next, of that user audience that will become aware of your product or service, how many will *engage* and *use* your product or service? Take the estimated total new users that the partnership would be responsible for and calculate what percentage it is of the entire existing user or customer base. How impactful will this partnership be to your company? Will it drive 20 percent more users? How much will the partnership increase the size of the pie? Do this same process to determine a revenue number and percentage of total revenue.

Also look through the lens of the internal functional team or group that this partnership is serving the most. This is your primary internal customer. You can determine who your primary internal customer is by way of the sub-metrics (the metrics that a functional group is responsible for) that the partnership will drive and impact. For example, does the partnership impact product metrics or marketing metrics? Or does the partnership accelerate an engineering schedule through the licensing of a technology that your engineering team no longer has to build on their own? Or does the partnership impact your sales organization's metrics by helping them reach a new market segment that they're not yet engaged with? Or maybe the partnership will help customer service by reducing call volume or increasing their Net Promoter Score (NPS) through a partnership? Your internal customer is paramount here, and understanding their needs and challenges is important to measure success. Get direct feedback from them on what metrics are most important, so you can get aligned on how the partnership is going to impact existing metrics.

If this partnership is to build your brand and create more awareness of your product, then sit down with your marketing team to understand how they gauge impact—for instance, perhaps they do it through direct traffic to your company website via input of your company's URL into search, not a paid search link. Or as part of the partnership, maybe you create a landing page or referral URL from the partner that you can track. Another key marketing metric is *earned media*, which is content published by a third party without any form of payment. When your company is mentioned in the press, like in an article about a new product launch or announcement, you're getting earned media. Tracking the number of articles your brand earns and how many times those articles are shared gives you an idea of the number of people your earned media efforts are reaching. Additional marketing metrics can include social engagement (interactions) and community reach (followers and likes).

Likewise, for product-related partnerships, understand from your product team what metrics they use to track product success. Some of the common metrics include usability and efficiency, which have to do with the ease of use of a product; frequency, which is how often users are coming back; and depth and engagement (time spent), which are about how long active users are engaging with your product in a given timeframe.

Once you've chosen your key metrics, identify what actions will impact those metrics and map out a timeline of improvement so you can monitor and manage the metrics throughout the partnership.

Also ensure you have a plan and agreement around business reporting related to the partnership initiatives, both from what content will be provided as well as how often. The business goals and objectives need to be reflected in the monthly or quarterly status reports, so ensure you have a way to provide the metrics that you and your partner SPOC need. For example, how are you tracking customer interest? How do you know marketing initiatives are driving in-store or website visits and ultimately purchases? Maybe you're using referral codes or another tracking technology. Once you get the data, visualize it in an easy-to-understand format for the core team and executives sponsoring the partnership. The data will drive decisions on how to move the partnership forward in context of the other initiatives that you and your internal team may be engaged in.

WHAT'S THE ROADMAP AND SCHEDULE?

Most likely the contractual agreement has already laid out a rough timeline with an estimated date for the targeted launch, and the Partnership Scope document should provide a broad roadmap of the key milestones. In the executing phase of the partnership, you can nail down more-specific dates by creating a shared work plan. A work plan is a clear execution plan based on the priorities. Without a solid, agreed-upon work plan, you won't have a clear direction for decision-making or guidance for when challenges arise along the way. You'll end up wasting a lot of time spinning your wheels instead of making forward progress.

Before the kickoff meeting, when meeting one-on-one with the SPOC counterpart, discuss and narrow the target launch date down from a quarter to a month to a week to a specific day. Determine the pros and cons of that date and why it may be better than others. Create a launch date recommendation. Get your executive sponsors to align on it, and then you can share that date with the core team.

Once you have a target launch date, work from that date to create a roadmap with a schedule of major milestones for the project calendar, including both shared tasks and independent tasks. First develop this joint schedule in a spreadsheet (or equivalent) so you and your SPOC can work on it together. Major milestones might include:

▸ Partnership kickoff session

▸ Initial alpha product (or service) demonstration

▸ Initial beta product (or service) demonstration

▸ Quality assurance and business approvals of initial beta release

▸ Beta launch (e.g., internal beta, friends and family beta, public beta)

▸ Public general launch to end customers

▸ Include target dates along with elapsed time for each of the major tasks, and be sure to adopt a program management process that works for both companies.

WHEN AND HOW OFTEN WILL YOU MEET?

Determine what the meeting schedule should be for the core team. A weekly call to start is good practice, and then you can change or update that plan over time. After discussing the meeting plan and agenda in the kickoff, send out the weekly meeting calendar invite.

Here are some tips for success in your core team meetings:

▶ Use a videoconferencing tool for the meetings to help with accountability and engagement. Be sure to encourage video is turned on.

▶ Develop an "Open Actions" list that is shared between the two teams and that will serve as the agenda for the weekly meetings. Publish the Open Actions list before and after the weekly meetings. Prior to the weekly call, action owners should have the opportunity to update their open items with the latest status.

▶ Program management tools can be evaluated as a way for the core teams to communicate and to coordinate tasks, but keep the weekly video call to ensure there are no surprises down the road with the partnership initiatives.

Besides the weekly meeting for the core team, also consider a weekly check-in with your SPOC. This gives you a chance to regularly assess what's working and what's not working. The point is not to paint a rosy picture; it's to identify and get out ahead of issues early. Those issues could be operational, relational, or anything that gets in the way of delivering the value you set out to create together. Establish a health score for the partnership. A simple green, yellow, and red stoplight works well. If the status is yellow or red, have details about why, including the action plan to remedy the situation.

Also come to an agreement with your SPOC on a quarterly business review schedule. These are meetings with your executive sponsors to provide a readout of the progress, highlighting issues and setting any expectations of what's coming next. Quarterly business reviews are a great time to refer back to your POP document. It provides a refresher for why you're going down the path of this partnership and allows you to check in with your counterpart on how the partnership is delivering on the identified objectives.

In your first quarterly business review, show the executive sponsors the core team roster, the meeting cadence, and the schedule with partnership milestones. Ask them if a quarterly meeting makes sense to them, and if the answer is yes, send out a recurring meeting invite. Discuss with your SPOC on the best way to send that calendar invite.

> **Show up early for your partner, metaphorically and literally.** When you lean in early for your partner, you show them that you care and are willing to work to help them achieve success, building trust and goodwill. Likewise, literally showing up early to meetings demonstrates respect. It's always better to be early than late.

ESTABLISH HOW INFORMATION WILL BE SHARED

One of the biggest challenges in partnerships is how to share information across companies. Not only are there the previously discussed confidentiality concerns, but companies use different software and tools that may not necessarily align.

Again, your legal team is your best friend. Your company may have strict policies about sharing information. Check with your legal team to get really clear about what information can be shared outside the walls of your company.

Then, determine *how* to share information so you can track progress and ensure you're executing against your goals. In my experience, simple, static documents, like Excel spreadsheets and Word documents, are most common. This allows you to manage what information is being shared and how it is edited.

Also consider how you will share information about the partnership internally. Communicating internally about the state and status of a partner relationship is key to success of any partnership. Internal stakeholders should always have a pulse on the general health of partnerships. This starts with identifying what communication methods work best within your company. There may already be a forum for you or others to update internal teams on the status of partnerships, including tools to easily communicate that status. If this is the situation, great. If not, figure out a way to provide regular updates about the general health of partnerships to stakeholders. Also include your "asks" for the internal team: what you need from them to move the partnerships to the right health status.

CREATE THE PARTNERSHIP EXECUTION PLAN

After the partnership kickoff meeting, create a Partnership Execution Plan document, which is a more in-depth, refined version of the Partnership Scope document. This document serves as a compass for the partnership, so take the time to write it. It should be a Microsoft Word or Google Docs file that lays out the scope, timeline, core team, and other key details for the partnering initiatives. This should be a *static* document, meaning it will not be constantly updated throughout the project timeline. It is meant to outline the initiatives at a high level. That way if, for example, a new team member joins the core team, they can first read the Partnership Execution Plan to get aligned and up to speed quickly. A key objective for the Partnership Execution Plan is to describe the context and intent of the partnership for all core team members. For a partnership to succeed, both teams need to believe in the initiative goals. The Partnership Execution Plan should clearly lay out the "why" of the partnership—the business context and reasons to do the project—as well as the "how."

A FOUNDATION FOR THE FUTURE

Managing a partnership can be incredibly challenging. You must bring together teams from different companies, with different cultures, values, and processes. On top of that, there's a good chance you're trying to create something completely new. The question isn't *if* issues and challenges will arise but *when*. To set yourself up for success, build strong relationships and establish clear operational guidelines. With a strong foundation, you will be able to build bigger and higher, so remember these key points:

▸ Understand and use the strengths each partner brings to the virtual partnership company. Creating a partnership is like creating a new company. Each partner should use each other's strengths as much as possible, including brand and marketing budget, to ensure the partnership is a success.

▸ Show up early for your partner, metaphorically and literally. When you lean in early for your partner, you show them that you care and are willing to work to help them achieve success, building trust and goodwill. Likewise, literally showing up early to meetings demonstrates respect. It's always better to be early than late.

In the final chapter of the book, we'll go over ways to evolve your partnerships and overall partnering strategy.

GROW: REACHING NEW HEIGHTS

CHAPTER 12

YOU HAVE A SUCCESSFUL PARTNERSHIP—NOW WHAT?

While I was working at an internet media company in 2004, we had a strategic partnership with a telecommunications company. We created a co-branded portal that took advantage of a great high-speed internet connection, with email, parental controls, and various other features that brought a premium experience of our web services to the telco's customers. For the telco's customers, it put everything in one easy-to-use place.

The nature of the telco market is that there are defined footprints, where certain telcos have access to certain homes, which means telcos are typically region based. After this initial strategic partnership, we started to understand the needs and challenges from other telcos around the world. We already had the initial partnership as our success story—a real and tangible example of our work—and we had also already developed the product experience. So we thought about how to extend that product value to cater to the needs of other telcos that were not in the same region of our initial partner. We ended up doing similar partnerships with several other telcos, creating a repeatable partner program that allowed us to scale our business in a predictable manner.

In addition to new partnerships, we also deepened our partnership with the first telco. At the time, they were interested in the "triple play," in which they provided a bundled services offering including high-speed internet, telephone services, and linear television. We aligned with them on this strategy and worked to bring an internet connected experience to a new screens beyond the PC: mobile phones and televisions. (You may recall that story from chapter 10, "Formalizing the Partnership and Deal.")

Basically, one partnership turned into many partnerships, both with our original partner and with new prospects. This is what stage 4, Grow, is all about: looking for creative ways to expand existing partnerships and grow ones. That typically happens in three ways:

- ▸ **Go deeper:** Do more within the established partnership area (a.k.a., progressing from crawl to walk to run).

- ▸ **Go broader:** Do other things with the partner, with new ideas or departments.

- ▸ **Go to others:** Do similar partnerships with other companies.

Let's dive into how to capitalize on your success (and even your failures) to create more partnerships and more growth.

CRAWL, WALK, RUN: BALANCING PRESENT AND FUTURE OPPORTUNITIES

As an initial partnership gets off the ground, part of your job is to uncover new opportunities for your company to pursue beyond the initial partner engagements. But remember to stay focused on the agreed-upon scope as the first priority. It's a balancing act of present and future opportunities. Remember: crawl, walk, run. If you try to rush ahead to running before you walk, you'll likely stumble and fall.

> **Don't get distracted, but build your parking lot.** There will always be lots of opportunities available to explore, but those explorations may not be aligned with your company's goals. Keep your objectives and priorities in mind while building the future scope for follow-on phases.

The initial project sets the tone for the partnership long term and requires your focus, but you can always start to think about what Phase 2 looks like. As you and the core teams are working through Phase 1, there may be times when certain features need to fall to a second or third priority due to the amount of time allocated in the schedule. This is where you start to build the Phase 2+ scope. Ensure you are in lockstep with your counterpart at the partner company around this process and determine what can be moved to after the Phase 1 launch. Depending on the urgency of the items, rather than calling it a Phase 2 scope and launch, you can create a plan for a fast-follow Phase 1.5 release. Ensure that your Phase 1 release has the core features to achieve the goals set forth in the initial agreement between you and the partner. If you did not put together the initial agreement, stay close to who did (e.g., the BD manager who negotiated and completed the term sheet and contract). Discuss any scope updates and the impacts and get their input on the trade-off and priorities that you're load balancing.

Ideally, Phase 1 naturally leads to Phase 2 leads to Phase 3. However, an initial partnership does not always lead to future partnering. Your partner may decide to "go at it alone" after an initial partnership. Sometimes they succeed, but in some cases, they fail and will come back to you, wanting to pick up where the partnership started or left off. Think back to why the partnership started in the first place. Did they not have the resources and technology to develop what your company had created? Were they looking to shift or evolve their brand in the minds of consumers? What's different now that they've come back? If nothing has changed and their company's partnering DNA is the same, you can either say no and walk away or ensure the terms this time around are more aligned to achieve successful outcomes for both parties from the partnership.

> **Keep hunting while gathering, and keep gathering while hunting.** Ensure there is a good balance of hunting and gathering, especially if you are responsible for both roles at your company. With continual hunting, if you and your partner go separate ways, you have other options, and with solid gathering, you may become more appealing to your existing partner and to future prospects.

Other times, you and your company may decide not to continue the partnership. Going deeper or broader with a partnership requires more investment. Before making that commitment, you should look back and evaluate the partnership to ensure it is still providing value.

THE PARTNERSHIP RETROSPECTIVE: LEARNING FROM YOUR FAILURES AND SUCCESSES

A partnership retrospective is when you look back on a partnership to assess what went right, what went wrong, and what lessons you can take away from it. As they say, hindsight is 20/20. When you're in the middle of a partnership, it can be hard to fully see what is happening. Taking the time for a retrospective allows you to learn from both your successes and failures, making you more effective at partnering in the future.

You should do a partnership retrospective every time a partnership phase is completed (so you would do a retrospective after the crawl phase, then again after the walk phase, and so on). You should do this retrospective internally and, if you intend to continue the partnership, externally with your partner as well. A retrospective helps to gain more clarity and alignment between you and your partner and also between your internal hunter and gatherer teams.

A partnership retrospective is also a great way to evaluate whether you should continue a partnership. For example, when I was working for an internet media company, I was leading a partnership with a top global technology company. The technology company had partnered with a TV manufacturer to put their own operating system into smart TVs, and we built a special app to ensure our service worked with their operating system. To put it bluntly, the project was a total failure. We poured a lot of time and money into creating the app and didn't get the expected result of reaching more users with our service.

A couple of years later, the technology company brought me another partnership idea: they were developing a new device for televisions, and they wanted us to build a special app experience for it. As you might imagine, I faced a lot of internal skepticism. The feeling was "We already tried a new project with them, and it didn't work. Why would we do it again?" Before I could answer that question, I needed to first answer a different question: *Why* didn't the first partnership work? Cue the partnership retrospective.

We'd actually already done a retrospective and had identified the big problem: the cost for consumers. They had to buy a special television to get the operating system, so it was just too expensive for broad consumer adoption. Our partner recognized that problem too. With this new device, they wanted to reach as wide of an audience as possible, so they were targeting a $35 price point. If we put our app on their device, it would be the lowest-cost way for users to access our service on a TV. This was a promising opportunity for us!

I held a town hall meeting and invited my partner contacts to come and demo the device. It was a tough crowd because of our earlier partnership failure, but by having the partner tell the story, provide the context, and show the device in action, we were able to shift people's perspectives. Still, we'd learned from the last partnership that we needed to structure the deal in a way to ensure our company would get a "win" from the partnership by reaching more consumers. The technology company agreed to pay for a three-month trial of our service for initial release, so we received a guaranteed amount of revenue for each device sold, plus the potential for future revenue if customers continued with their subscription. With the free trial, the device practically paid for itself, so it flew off the shelves. Our partner sold a lot of devices, we attracted a lot of new customers, and the partnership was a resounding success.

If we hadn't done a partnership retrospective, we might have refused to continue working with this partner, which would have been a mistake. Even if a partnership is a failure, it can prove valuable in the long run—as long as you learn from it. Don't let the successes make you complacent either. Partnering is an ever-evolving art form. Factors around you will change, from technological advancements to economic and political climates. There are so many variables that can shift, which means you can't know everything. So be a sponge and keep learning. This is how you'll grow and continue to hone the craft of business partnerships.

FINDING YOUR PARTNERING RECIPE

Over time in a company's growth evolution, there is a recalibration exercise of what efforts and activities are truly moving the needle for your company. After one or two successful partnerships have shown tangible impact to your company, your executive team or board may start asking, "Can we do another of those partnerships?" or "Can we do more with partnering?" You want these questions to arise, but DD teams are not order takers. They are strategic and critical thinkers that synthesize various business factors, market signals, relationship health, and other ingredients to develop the right *partnering recipes*.

A recipe is not created on the first try. You have to make it several times, testing and tweaking until it tastes just right. Then it's called a recipe. Likewise, with each partnership you do, you can test and optimize until you create your own partnering recipes: the partnering strategies that you know work to deliver impact and that make the most sense for your business.

Creating a partnering recipe starts with having a clear picture of the impact of your partnerships. Once you have a few partnerships under your belt, create an internal Partner Performance dashboard and do a side-by-side comparison to better understand your various partnerships' relative impact. Categorize your partners into relevant buckets to ensure you're comparing apples to apples, so to speak, and start by looking at the partnerships' impact to your North Star metric.

For example, when I worked on partnerships with a global entertainment company, our North Star metric was monthly viewing hours. After two-plus years of engaging with more than seventy partners, we analyzed the data and found that about five partners were driving roughly 80 percent of the monthly viewing hours, and the remaining 20 percent was made up of fifty-plus partners with very low viewing hours. At the time, our team's level of effort was evenly distributed across all partners, with some extra focus on the obvious big names. After analyzing the data, we decided to invest more in those five most impactful partners and explore an alternative approach to address the other partners.

As you analyze the data, you may find that your team's level of effort is the same across every partner in the same category regardless of the business impact. That's okay. You're figuring things out. You can adjust moving forward.

Your North Star metric is the most important, but keep other important metrics in mind as well. In the above example, the fifty-plus partners with smaller impact were not all created equal. Some were strategic bets, and we had strong reasons to partner with them beyond viewing hours. For example, some helped with international expansion in key territories, and others involved new innovations in mobile video experiences, which presented learning opportunities as well as new ways to reach new audiences and demographics.

Based on the data, you can start determining your partnering recipe—what types of partnerships have the most impact—so you know what additional partners you might want to hunt. As you adjust your larger partnering strategy, share it with your internal stakeholders. Help them see the big picture of all the partnerships you're pursuing and how partnering is key to the business's success, so that they will continue to support your partnering strategy and ideas.

PARTNER PROGRAMS: WHAT ARE THEY AND WHEN SHOULD YOU DO THEM?

So far, the type of partnerships we've discussed are *strategic partnerships*, bespoke relationships largely built from the ground up to fit a specific prospect. That's what my team and I did when we created the co-branded portal with our first major telco partner. As you do strategic partnerships and figure out your partnering recipe, you can begin to explore and develop partner programs, which are a more turnkey approach and can before more self-serve for prospects over time. From the telco example, the subsequent partnerships we formed after the initial strategic partnership would be considered a partner program. We didn't need to build new portals from the ground up—we turned the work we'd already done into a platform that could be used by multiple partners.

Partner programs can be extremely powerful and company-changing if done right. They provide a preset formula for engaging with partners: there are set business terms for the partner program agreement, a set timeline for the initial engagement to launch, and a set process to ensure your prospect is aware of what's happening each step of the way. Since so much of the partnership is preset, you can save a lot of time and effort, allowing you to scale your partnering strategy.

IS A PARTNER PROGRAM RIGHT FOR YOU?

What drives the need for a partner program is the market need. So start with understanding prospect segmentation in the market.

Within a given market, you often have two types of prospects: whales and tunas. Whales are the really big, impactful partners—if you catch a whale, you can step-change your business. Tunas are smaller partners that have less individual impact, but if you add them all up, you can match the impact of the whale partner. Both whales and tunas have value and are worth pursuing. The challenge is how to cater to the tunas in a scalable way, without using the same amount of effort for every tuna that you use for each whale. Usually, this leads to a bifurcation of strategic partnerships (for the whales) and partner programs (for the tunas).

Set up the criteria for what is a whale and what is a tuna for your business. Are there two to three whales and then all the rest are tunas? How big is the market opportunity for the whales, the tunas, and the entire market segment? Your answers will help to size the quantity of customers and the low- to high-touch engagements that may or may not be possible to develop programs for.

Now determine your company's win-win value proposition for those prospect segments. Often, partner programs will evolve from strategic partnerships, so look at any partnerships you've already put together and what value your company is providing. For example, did you create something new on the product front for your partner to integrate with your platform more easily? Would other companies benefit from this type of partnership? Are there others prospects facing the same issues as your current partner? Can you envision at least two to four other partners utilizing the same type of experience that was developed for your first partner?

Think of the elements of the partnership engagement that can be repeated and provided in a one-to-many way. This could include branding on the product or a design template for partners to select from. You and your product and technical teams can determine what to offer to the different tiers of your partners and what custom work could be built into tools and managed simultaneously when multiple partners are using the same platform. (That's what we did in the previous telco example.)

As you consider a partner program, make sure you're not impacting your relationships with existing partners. Can you expand this type of partnership to other prospects without causing business or strategy conflict with your company? If you have a value proposition that will resonate with several companies and you can work with multiple partners taking into account contractual, legal and regulatory, and relationship considerations, a partner program could be a good option for you.

CREATING A PARTNER PROGRAM

You need to launch a partner program for one to exist, but that doesn't mean you have to do everything all at once. Just as you approach strategic partnerships from a "crawl, walk, run" mindset, do the same thing with partner programs.

▶ **Phase 1—Crawl:** Either start with a bespoke strategic partnership that will serve as the framework for the partner program, or start by building the partner program model to serve end customers and then determine how to position that offering externally.

▶ **Phase 2—Walk:** Develop platform capabilities and tools that allow more than one prospect to engage with the products and test the program out with a limited set of pilot partners.

▶ **Phase 3—Run:** After you test, learn, and optimize the partner program with your pilot partners, roll it out to a broader audience.

To make the business case for a partner program, create an outlook for the potential opportunity in aggregate: the total number of customers you can engage based on all the partners the program could serve.

When designing a partner program, outline these key areas in detail:

▶ **Who is responsible for what:** Provide clarity around the scope of work and which party does what in the process. There are distinct roles in managing a partner program. There is the partner manager or partner program manager who is responsible for the actual relationships with external companies or developers, and then there are the product team members who are responsible for the program from a product perspective, including the features and tools and how those serve the needs for those partners.

▶ **What the process is:** Outline a predictable process from concept to launch, including major milestones. Remove the complexity from the process and make it as simple as possible.

▶ **How the project will be managed:** What tools and resources will be used throughout the project for support, issue tracking, quality assurance, and so on? How often will you meet and talk through the status of the partnership, and what is the ongoing agenda for those meetings? Think about and assess self-serve approaches to help with scaling. For example, partnership-facing online tools can serve as a "source of truth" for documentation around a partner engagement, from processes to schedules to best practices.

Keep in mind that a partner program is a living thing. As you move through the crawl, walk, and run stages, it will continue to build on itself in order to cater to the needs of your target prospects.

ELEVATING A PARTNER PROGRAM

The disadvantage to a partner program is that the partnerships can all start to look the same. They become cookie-cutter partnerships instead of strategic ones. But it doesn't have to be that way. Try to have a level of customization to make each partnership unique, and while a partnership may start as part of a partner program, you can look for creative ways to go deeper or broader.

THE CONTINUAL PARTNERING JOURNEY

The Co-Elevate Method isn't a one-and-done process. It is a continual, ever-evolving strategy. Remember: the Co-Elevate Method provides a foundation so that, using your judgment, you can navigate through your unique situation and apply the tools and strategies that are helpful.

With every partnership, you will learn valuable lessons that help you to grow and partner more effectively.

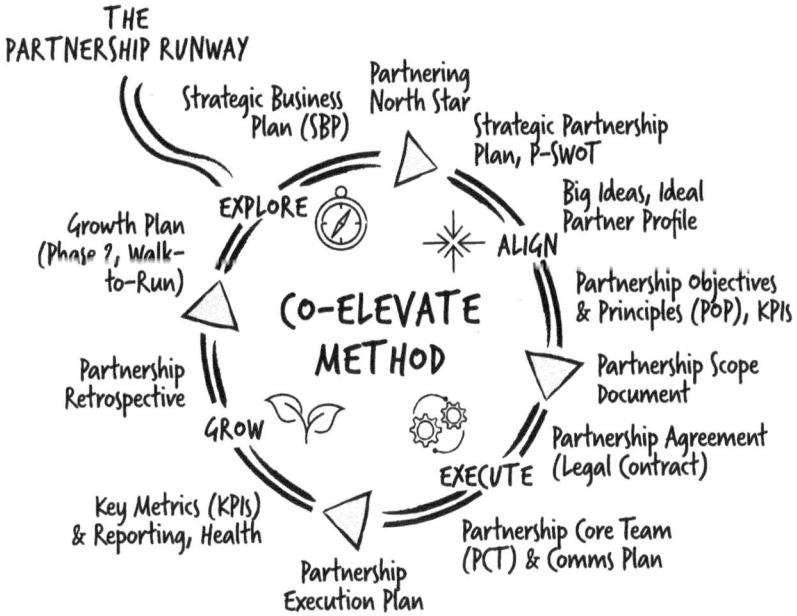

Keep these final tips in mind as you grow your Co-Elevate Partnerships:

▸ **Don't get distracted, but build your parking lot.** There will always be lots of opportunities available to explore, but those explorations may not be aligned with your company's goals. Keep your objectives and priorities in mind while building the future scope for follow-on phases.

▸ **Keep hunting while gathering, and keep gathering while hunting.** Ensure there is a good balance of hunting and gathering, especially if you are responsible for both roles at your company. With continual hunting, if you and your partner go separate ways, you have other options, and with solid gathering, you become more appealing to your existing partner and to future prospects.

THE FUTURE OF PARTNERSHIPS

For practically all of history, humans have relied on partnerships. From hunting woolly mammoths to building architectural wonders to making world-changing scientific and technological breakthroughs—it is through working together that we achieve greatness.

As technology changes and consumer expectations grow higher and higher, partnerships are only going to become more necessary to deliver transformative outcomes. The people and companies that do partnerships well are the ones that will survive and thrive.

It's bigger than that, though. Partnerships don't just benefit the companies involved. They benefit all of us. Through partnerships, we can advance innovation across many industries—

technology, energy, education, medicine, and more—and help humanity progress faster and farther. We can co-elevate not just people and companies, but the world at large.

Isaac Newton said, "If I have seen further, it is by standing on the shoulders of giants." This is true for me as well. I've been fortunate to be a part of a variety of companies, business cultures, and partnership initiatives, and I've learned from a number of excellent business and BD leaders. I can see further because of those who came before me, and in this book, I've worked to distill decades of knowledge so that you can see even further—or, if you're a BD and partnerships veteran, so that you can see from additional perspectives. If you're a veteran, you may have your own process and methodology, and I would love to connect with you to learn about your approaches and collaborate to help our future generations of BD and partnerships professionals.

Partnering isn't an exact science. It always requires some improvisation, and the content of this book is best learned through life experience and on-the-job training. I believe if more companies and teams use and adapt a common partnering framework there can be a more a successful path to realizing and sustaining impactful strategic partnerships. If you have found the content in this book to be valuable, I urge you to share this book with your prospects and partners to discuss and align how to adapt the Co-Elevate Method for your next partnership together. As you take these principles and strategies and make them your own, you will gain your own wisdom, and one day, others will stand upon your shoulders. I look forward to what you will build through strategic partnerships and how you will help others.

I believe embracing a common partnering mindset and methodology can develop a network effect across teams, companies, and industries accelerating the number of high quality partnerships that rise the tide of innovation, business growth, and consumer value on a global scale—that's a grand vision and I hope you and others reading this book can get us there.

CONCLUSION

From start-ups to Fortune 500 companies, partnerships are the future, and the future of partnerships starts with *you*. I thank you for your time, your energy, and your consideration of the ideas and shared learnings set forth in this book. I hope this book helps you to do your life's best work, as the best is yet to come. Let's partner and Co-Elevate!

Have questions or comments? I want to hear about
your partnering situations, challenges, and wins.
You can connect with me at: linkedin.com/in/richezekiel
or visit www.coelevatebook.com.

INDEX

www.ingramcontent.com/pod-product-compliance
Lightning Source LLC
Chambersburg PA
CBHW041551240326
41458CB00148BB/6836/J